THE FAMILY BUSINESS

MANAGEMENT HANDBOOK

FROM THE EDITORS OF
FAMILY BUSINESS MAGAZINE

Family Business Publishing Co., Philadelphia • 1996

THE FAMILY BUSINESS MANAGEMENT HANDBOOK

Editor: Mark Fischetti

Design: Bill Cooke

Advisors: Charles E. Fiero, Howard Muson

Production: Christine van Dyke

Editorial assistants: Myrna Carson,
   JoAnne Redding, Keren Weiner

FAMILY BUSINESS PUBLISHING CO.

Chairman: Milton L. Rock

Co-Chairman: Charles E. Fiero

President: Robert H. Rock

ISBN 0-9673745-3-7

Published June 1996
Second Printing June 1997
Third Printing July 1998
Fourth Printing August 2000

The Best of the New Management Wisdom

THE PAST DECADE has witnessed the phenomenal growth of a new field devoted to helping owners of family businesses better manage their companies. One indication of this rapid development is the more than 100 university forums that have sprung up across the United States to bring family owners together with the diversity of professionals who advise and study this type of company.

No doubt the primary stimulus has been demographic: Many of the countless businesses born after World War II are now facing problems in transferring leadership to a new generation. Contrary to their popular image, these companies are not only "mom-and-pop" businesses. As recent surveys have shown, a sizable number are highly professionalized, multimillion-dollar enterprises constantly reaching out for new ways to improve their operations and stay competitive.

We now have a growing body of knowledge about the family owned and family controlled company. In six years of publication, *Family Business* Magazine has been reporting on and interpreting this knowledge for you, the business owner. In this time, the editors have been impressed with one truth: The principles of management taught in most business schools do not always apply to the family business. No matter what the size of the company, the "family factor" subtly (and sometimes disastrously) influences almost every major function, from marketing to accounting, and virtually all major decisions, from how the company will be organized to its rate of new investment and expansion.

This Handbook is designed to help you manage the complex interaction between family and business and assist you in your efforts to create a more efficient, profitable, and harmonious company. Rather than a collection of articles, it is a "how-to" manual that distills from the pages of 40 issues of *Family Business* the best advice of an array of top-flight experts as well as family business leaders such as you.

The book is divided into six sections. Section I deals with the unique challenges of leadership and strategy in a family firm. Section II is concerned with managing family relationships, improving communication, and heading off conflict in the business. Section III provides data on compensation in family firms as well as tips on incentives for family and nonfamily managers.

The fourth section suggests many of the ways you can improve operations within the context of a family business; it includes pieces on strengthening customer service and marketing, on featuring your family in advertising, on competitive intelligence, and on reengineering a family company. Section V tells you how to go about organizing a board and recruiting the best team of advisors for your business. The sixth section covers aspects of the No. 1 challenge—succession—offering specific advice on such basic tasks as mentoring the next generation and retirement planning. Finally, we have appended a section listing some resources for readers who want to delve deeper into some of these topics.

Léon Danco, the founding father of family business consulting and one of our regular *Family Business* columnists, has for years been urging his clients to put up a sign in their offices saying: "This business shall go on forever." The Editors of *Family Business* hope this Handbook will help you keep that promise to your family, and fulfill the promise of your business for generations to come.

Howard Muson

Editor & Publisher, *Family Business* Magazine

Contributors

The editors would like to thank the following family business experts, owners, and writers who have contributed to this book. Their insightful work was originally prepared for Family Business *magazine, and appears on the pages indicated.*

Benjamin Benson, consultant, Boynton Beach, FL: p. 45

Alec Berkman, Financial Kinetics Corp., Pomona, CA: p. 59

Barbara B. Buchholz and Margaret Crane, writers, La Due, MO: p. 21

Mike Cohn, Cohn Financial Group, Phoenix, AZ: pp. 102, 112, 117

Edwin T. Crego Jr., TQS Group, Chicago, IL: pp. 38, 45, 49, 115

Léon Danco, Center for Family Business, Cleveland, OH: pp. 28, 47, 48, 114

Jeffrey S. Davis, Mage Centers for Management Development, Wellesley, MA: p. 22

François de Visscher, de Visscher & Co., Greenwich, CT: p. 31

Peter Davis, Pulsar Equity Partners, W. Conshohocken, PA: pp. 6, 10, 16, 30, 42, 44, 90, 93, 95

Ronald Drucker, attorney, Philadelphia, PA: p. 45

David W. Ewing, writer, Boston, MA: p. 24

Mark Fischetti, Family Business Magazine, Philadelphia, PA: pp. 26, 60

Anne B. Fisher, Fortune Magazine, New York, NY: p. 72

Tom Garbett, Doremus & Co., New York, NY: p. 73

Joe M. Goodman, Holton Howard Goodman P.C., Nashville, TN: p. 103

Barbara Hollander, (in memorium): p. 40

Tom Hubler, Hubler Family Business Consultants, Minneapolis, MN: p. 29

Donald J. Jonovic, Family Business Management Services, Cleveland, OH: p. 91

Kenneth Kaye, psychologist, Skokie, IL: pp. 35, 56

Richard F. Lane, Ludwig Bulmer Seifert & Lane, Hackensack, NJ: p. 78

Ivan Lansberg, Lansberg Associates, New Haven, CT: pp. 94, 97, 108, 115

Gerald Le Van, Le Van Associates, Black Mountain, NC: p. 94

Lila Lewey and Stephen B. Swartz, McGladrey & Pullen, Minneapolis, MN: p. 12

Stan Luxenberg, writer, New York, NY: p. 64

Andrea Grace Mackiewicz, writer, New York, NY: p. 43

G. Jeff Mennen, G.J. Mennen Group, Florham, NJ: p. 8

Louis Moscatello, analyst, Great Barrington, MA: p. 99

Howard Muson, Family Business Magazine, Philadelphia, PA: pp. 66, 80

John S. Powell, Family Business Mediation Services, Burlington, NC: p. 36

Karen Sindelar, Coopers & Lybrand LLP, San Francisco, CA: p. 52

Baker A. Smith, Morris-Anderson Assoc. Ltd., Atlanta, GA: p. 85

Marcy Syms, Syms Corp., Secaucus, NJ : p. 17

John L. Ward, Loyola University, Chicago, IL: p. 92

Scott Ward, University of Pennsylvania, Philadelphia, PA: p. 69

CONTENTS

Continued...

CONTENTS

Continued

Family Business

Where to find the answers when your management questions involve the "family factor"

Like other premier business publications, *Family Business* tackles tough management problems. But unlike the others, we also consider the "family factor" (that set of circumstances unique to company owners who are related to each other).

Family Business fills a critical information gap for managing family companies like yours. There is no other unbiased resource that recognizes the subtle interplay of business and family and offers guidance accordingly.

A magazine *and* subscriber-only archive access

A one-year *Family Business* subscription includes:

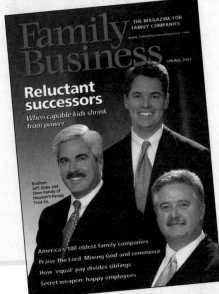

1. Four quarterly issues of the magazine and — at no additional charge —

2. Subscriber-only access to our complete archive/information database at **www.familybusinessmagazine.com**.

An incredible treasure trove of content

Family Business Magazine covers virtually every subject of importance to family company stakeholders. Published since 1989, it provides tried-and-true solutions and practical management tips with feature articles written by the field's top experts and real-life accounts by enterprise owners like yourself.

Solid content like this makes the searchable online archive/information database an incredible treasure trove. Here's a sampling from the list of almost 80 topics you can choose:

- Buy-Sell Agreements
- Compensation & Benefits
- Conflict Resolution
- Cousin Co-management
- Estate Planning
- Gifting

- Mentoring
- Non-family Managers
- Shareholder Liquidity
- Sibling Partnerships
- Succession Planning
- Valuation

For quick reference or in-depth study

Whatever your industry, whatever your size, when your management questions involve the "family factor," you can find the answers at **www.familybusinessmagazine.com.**

Twelve years of *Family Business* magazine articles (literally hundreds) are indexed and on our website right now. The content of each new issue is posted as soon as it's published; expert advice and counsel from other carefully selected sources are added weekly to ensure constant enrichment and continuous expansion.

Most importantly, you can get what you want when you want it — easily and quickly — one article or many — even if computer is not your first language.

Exclusively for you, the lowest rate available

A *Family Business* subscription regularly sells for $95. We invite you to try *Family Business* now for the special low price: 1 year for just $79.

You'll receive four quarterly issues of *Family Business* Magazine, each packed with 80 pages of hard-hitting management information. You'll also get (to use whenever you want, as often as you want, for one full year) your personal access codes to the subscriber-only online archive/information database (see sample web pages above).

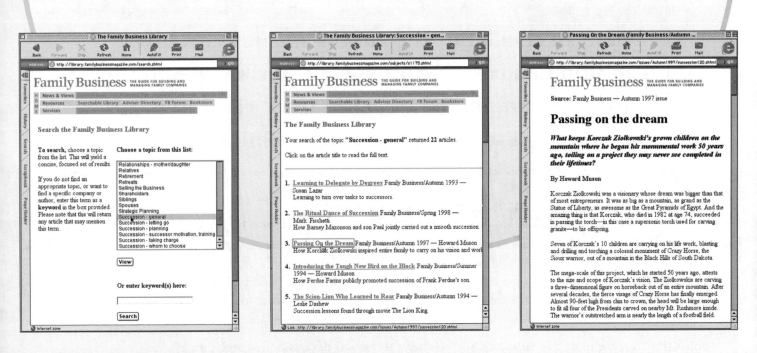

Visit the *Family Business* archive/information database just once to pinpoint your answer, clarify your issues or identify your options and your $79 annual subscription will pay for itself in 10 minutes. Keep using the database throughout the year and you'll be home free every time!

PLUS: More offers for subscribers only

As a subscriber to *Family Business*, you can get the lowest prices (up to a 25% discount off the regular price) on every volume of our management handbook series, including:

> *The Family Business Management Handbook, The Family Business Succession Handbook, The Family Business Leadership Handbook, Building Strong Family Teams, Financial Management of Your Family Company*, and our newest publication, *The Family Business Compensation Handbook*.

With this iron-clad Guarantee

If *Family Business* doesn't live up to your expectations for any reason, you can cancel your subscription and receive an immediate refund for all unmailed issues. *Family Business* extends this guarantee on all publications. No questions asked. Period.

Subscribe now

Please take a moment right now to subscribe to *Family Business*. Simply complete and fax the order form on the following page to 215-405-6078. Or order securely online at: **www.familybusinessmagazine.com.**

The first of your four quarterly issues of *Family Business* Magazine will be sent to you right away — along with your personal access codes to the online archive/information database.

Want to check out the *Family Business* archive/
information database *before* you subscribe? Be our guest.
You can sample the treasure trove right now at
www.familybusinessmagazine.com

The Family Business Subscription Order Form

☑ **YES,** I want to subscribe to *Family Business* at $79 for one year. I understand my
subscription will include four quarterly issues of the magazine and unlimited access to the
Family Business online archive/information database.

Send the first issue of my subscription and my personal access codes right away.

I understand that I may cancel my subscription at any time and receive a prompt refund for all
unmailed copies — guaranteed.

❑ My check for $79 is enclosed.

    ❑ Please charge my: ❑ AMEX   ❑ VISA   ❑ MasterCard

Card # _____ **Expiration Date** _____

Signature _____

Print Name _____ Position _____

Company _____

Mailing Address _____

City _____

State /Province _____ **ZIP/Postal Code** _____ **Country** _____

Phone _____ Fax _____

E-mail _____ ▬▬▬▬▬▬▬▬

   HB

Please **fax** this completed form with credit card payment to *Family Business*: **215-405-6078**
Or subscribe securely at **www.familybusinessmagazine.com**
Or **mail** the form to *Family Business*, P.O. Box 41966, Philadelphia, PA 19101-1966
Or **call** 800-637-4464 or 215-567-3200

For Canadian and Mexican subscriptions add $10 for postage. All other countries add $30.
Remittances in U.S. dollars only.

Family Business: Where to find the answers
when your management questions involve the "family factor"

— I —

LEADERSHIP

◆———

FIRST AND FOREMOST, the men and women who run the best family businesses are exceptional leaders. Indeed, no business can succeed without strong leadership. That is why this book begins with advice on how to lead a family business.

Great leaders craft a vision for their business and develop a strategy to meet it. The first chapter examines how noteworthy family business leaders created dynamic visions and long-range plans. It also presents what one well-known leader sees as the greatest challenges facing family business owners in the coming decade.

Because spouses, children, and relatives are involved, few family business leaders choose to be dictators. They build management teams comprising family and nonfamily employees, and generate company-wide support for them. All enlightened corporations are moving in the same management direction. How to erect and sustain these valuable teams is discussed in Chapter 2.

Leaders and executive teams with long track records eventually have to transfer their knowledge and experience to successors. Chapter 3 offers practical advice on passing along leadership capabilities—from a founder to a son, and from the second generation to the third.

Strategy and Vision

Developing a dynamic plan

To be a market leader, you need long-range goals—and a strategy for implementing them. Here's how to get started.

IN THE HISTORY OF FAMILY BUSINESSES, there are countless examples of great leaders who have come along in the second, third, or fourth generations and transformed a modest family business into an enormously successful enterprise. Frank Perdue built an empire from his parents' small chicken business. John Searle at G.D. Searle was third generation, as were the Dayton brothers at Dayton Hudson; the current Nordstroms are third generation, and Gussie Busch of Anheuser-Busch was fourth. In each case the leader saw an opening in the marketplace, a "loose brick" in the competitive wall, and by driving a wedge into it was able to build the business by several orders of magnitude.

These great success stories provide us with insight on what keeps family businesses alive and well. Clear vision and a well-articulated strategy have been central to every one. A long-range plan specifies where you want to be in a few years. A strategy spells out how you intend to get there.

When Nordstrom Inc. started to become a major force in department store retailing, the family was powerfully committed to growth, success, and leadership. Their strategy was to go after high-end consumers, offering them extraordinary product quality, merchandising, and service at a full retail price. To set high standards of service, they had to find a select group of motivated salespeople who would be dedicated to customer service. They had to establish a highly talented merchandising team and bruisingly tough standards for their suppliers. Every element of their strategy reinforced the other and spelled out where fanatical attention to detail was needed.

Unfortunately, most family firms don't seem to have a strategy. Too many are hanging in there by the grace of God, just managing to survive year after year. They know

their businesses and their customers well. They know how to sell at a price. But they don't know how to compete for long-term survival. Part of the problem is that, too often, family companies do not change with the times, because of a family stalemate or because the "loyal" management unshakingly resists change.

The examples cited above are of transformational strategies. In each case, the industry was changing and market leaders were slow in adapting to that change. Newcomers seized the high ground by moving swiftly to fill an unmet customer need. Perdue, Apple Computer, Nordstrom, Wal-Mart, and Jacuzzi all grew by means of breakthrough strategies. They all had a better mousetrap and were in the right place at the right time.

Jacuzzi provides an interesting example of how a breakthrough strategy emerges in a family business. Roy Jacuzzi was about the 105th family member to have been employed by his family's plumbing business in California. What Jacuzzi saw was the unmet need for the product that now bears the family name. In developing that product he not only transformed his family business—he transformed an industry.

In some industries today, change is so rapid that the strategic choices are simply to grow, sell, or perish. The drug distribution business, along with many other distribution businesses, has been going through a period of rapid consolidation. Economies of scale have developed that make it virtually impossible for the small company to compete. In 15 years the number of companies in the industry has gone from 300 to 50; roughly 250 family businesses have been sold or have gone out of business.

A few family businesses saw the trend and moved quickly to buy up other companies, staying ahead of the pack. One example is Bergen-Brunswick, which the Martini brothers built into a $4 billion-dollar-a-year enterprise. Some other pretty smart operators waited until the consolidation wave grew and then sold their businesses just as the acquisition fever was at its peak (making a bundle). Those who were asleep at the switch during this period missed out.

Distribution has become a game for giants. Most of the niches in the business have been wiped out by technology. But fortunately, this is not the norm. There are many industries today in which niches in the marketplace are surviving and flourishing. The demand for specialty in everything from food to bookstores has grown dramatically. Family businesses that occupy a niche, even in a dull market, can do very well. Many have built their franchise over several generations—L.L. Bean, Smucker's, Lemme's chocolates, for example. These niche businesses often are highly profitable but, almost by definition, limited in size. Their key to strategy for niche businesses is to preserve customer loyalty by paying scrupulous attention to quality and service, while keeping the competition out of the niche.

Niches can be easily lost, however. This possibility should prompt the niche player to diversify. The company needs to use its resources to buy into other businesses and learn to operate them before the cash cow is squeezed dry. (Some companies are so nervous about losing their niche that they constantly ask: "Should we cash out now, while we can still get top dollar?") Again, timing is everything.

A few fortunate family companies are market leaders in their industries and they face their own strategic challenge—how to maintain leadership. Some of the biggest are Milliken, Steelcase, and Anheuser-Busch, but many mid-size firms also lead their markets. A major threat to market leaders is "cherry picking." A competitor comes along and picks out the best market segments, leaving the market leader with the least attractive segments. Another threat is that the market leader will be dethroned by a competitor's technological breakthrough. Timex, for example, was quickly upended from its leading position in the watch market by Japanese electronic watch technology. But the biggest threat to market leaders is that they will lose touch with the marketplace: become too big, too homogeneous, too bureaucratic to survive.

A successful strategy for a market leader involves what Steelcase's chairman, Robert C. Pew, once described as

Generate family consensus. Then flank the competition or engage in guerrilla warfare.

"demassification." That strategy calls for breaking up the bureaucracy, decentralizing operations, adding uniqueness to the offerings in each market segment, and improving response time to changing customer needs. Market leaders have to confront the little guys who try to take away their business. They must have a product, a price, and a service for every segment of the market; if they don't, they may leave gaps for other companies to fill. And they must avoid overpricing in any segment, lest they give the impression of gouging and stimulate a competitor to stampede customers with lower prices.

A market leadership strategy can be expensive. Steelcase, a third-generation family business, has poured more than $400 million into the process of demassification, raising some speculation that it may go into debt. Yet the plight of General Motors clearly shows us the fate of market leaders who don't make the necessary investment and changes.

If family businesses have any intrinsic advantage, it is their ability to plan for the long run. Most shareholders are patient, and in most family firms management doesn't have to worry too much about losing control. But this intrinsic advantage is useless unless it is acted upon. Every family business needs a long-range vision and a strategy. The vision can be general, but it must be specific enough in key areas to provide a sense of direction.

The family's vision for the future of the company should be generated by family consensus. For some the vision is to be a global company; for others, it's to dominate a niche. For still others, it's to be a market leader. A strategy shows how the firm plans to achieve the vision. Will it confront the competition, flank it, or engage in guerrilla warfare? What will be its product strategy, and in what markets will it choose to compete? A long-range plan takes months to put together, but a strategy can be formulated in a day. With a vision, patient investors, and a smart strategy, even the most resource-constrained competitor can conquer the world.

— Peter Davis

Five challenges for the '90s... and beyond

G. Jeff Mennen, a one-time vice-chairman of the 113-year-old Mennen Company, forsees significant perils for family firms as they move into the future. The family sold the firm in 1992 because diverging interests in the fourth generation could not be satisfied any other way. Forewarned is forearmed.

THE MENNEN COMPANY was started in 1872 and grew to a multimillion-dollar enterprise marketing aftershave, deodorant, and baby products in more than 100 countries. My role in the family company began in 1964, when I started as a sales trainee in Washington, D.C. I ran our international division for 10 years. Before becoming vice-chairman in 1981, I was in charge of bringing newly acquired firms into the company and teaching them about the Mennen Co. culture.

For years, people I met said, "You work in a family business? Oh, that's nice. You have nothing much to do, you've got it made." During the last 10 to 15 years, however, people have come to realize the importance of family businesses to the U.S. economy. Family owned companies have probably been responsible for most of the major innovative products of the past 50 years. We provide more than 65 percent of the GNP and more than 50 percent of our nation's jobs. We give tremendous stability to the work force. Anyone who doubts that can look at how many of the public-company mergers and LBOs of the 1980s have been going down the tubes and figure how many jobs have been lost as a result.

Family businesses have been, and will continue to be, the backbone of the economy, and that's something we should all be proud of. But that doesn't mean that we don't face significant perils as we move into the future.

There are five major challenges facing family businesses in the 1990s, three of them from outside economic forces and two from strains inherent in the process of assuring continuity of family ownership.

The first outside challenge is from competitors, who are consolidating. In almost every industry, a few companies are getting bigger and stronger, and they are aiming their guns at family business. That means you have to be smarter: To beat the competitive pressures in your markets, you have to manage your businesses more scientifically than before. In the '90s the battle is price versus service. For the most part, family owned companies are not able to compete with their giant competitors on price alone. The key to success, then, is service. Do a better job for your customer and you win the battle.

The second major outside challenge comes from your biggest corporate customers, who are also consolidating. They are working to achieve their own goals, which may not be consistent with your goals. Their goal is to get the price down to the lowest level, while protecting their profits. The squeeze has to come somewhere, and you are the "squeezee." Family owned businesses have to develop a plan to keep from getting squeezed out. Find a way to become more important to these customers. Look at service and dependability.

A third major challenge is that family business owners are going to have to look to nontraditional sources of funding for growth. You know that you have to grow to stay alive, and that is an important message to pass down to future generations. It is difficult to get loans to finance expansion. We must pursue other sources of financing, be they pension funds, insurance companies, private family offices, or commercial firms.

The inside challenges may be more difficult to deal with because they involve intense emotions as well as reason and logic. Of course, the biggest challenge is developing plans to turn over the reins to the next generation. We had a 10-year program for my family to accomplish such a transition at the Mennen Co. I emphasize the 10-year period because I have learned that these transitions can't be done overnight.

You might think that a 113-year-old company learned from experience methods of planning and carrying out a smooth succession. Unfortunately, that wasn't the case. My company's history began with my great-grandfather, who was the second son of a ship-owning, seafaring German family. He came to America when he was 14 years old, with no money. After going through pharmacy school, he opened up his own pharmacy where he made corn plasters, talcum powders, and shampoos for anyone who would buy them locally in the Newark area. The business was duly handed over to my grandfather.

My grandfather, William G. Mennen, ran our business and our family with an iron hand for well over 65 years and finally let go of the reins in 1963—or, rather, he loosened his grip on the reins. His hold on the company was so persistent that there was a board meeting in his hospital room on the day he died in 1968. He was 84.

During my grandfather's tenure, the Mennen Co. became what it is today. Mennen Skin Bracer, the first men's aftershave on the U.S. market, became the No. 1 brand sold in this country and a strong seller throughout the Western World. We also introduced our deodorants and Mennen Baby Magic line on my grandfather's watch.

My grandparents had four children, two daughters and two sons. The girls were told in no uncertain terms that their job in life was to do charity work, make babies, and keep quiet. When time came for succession planning, however, my father thought he would create a little excitement in the family: He passed over his oldest son and named his second son, my father, as president of the company.

During my father's years as head of the business, we became a truly international company. The impetus for our moves into foreign markets came largely from U.S. tax laws. We needed to expand our business in order not to get taxed more, and the international marketplace provided us with the avenue to do this.

In the 1980s our company was led by a nonfamily CEO and chairman, L. Donald Horn. For the last 10 years, I have been engaged with our family in attempting to plan for future leadership transitions. The reason I got involved was that I could see my family had done such a good job of keeping people in my generation out of the business that I was the only one in management. (My sister and one of my two brothers worked in nonmanagement positions.) I did not want that to happen in the fifth generation of the company.

I realized that there was going to come a time when I did not have the older generation to counsel me. I sought help.

Guided by the best consulting advice I could find, we started a three-pronged program to plan for the future. The first prong was to get the older generation, my father and his siblings, to loosen up on the reins. The second prong was to educate members of my generation, as owners and board members, in our responsibilities to the company, to our parents, and to the next generation. And the third prong was to start trying to interest members of the fifth generation in joining the company.

The process should have begun 15 years earlier with the older generation. One of their biggest concerns is life after the business. They ask: "What happens to my status among peers when I am retired and they aren't? What happens to my status in the community, my company perks? How do I handle this change in life at my age? Do I just roll over and die?"

We spend a lot of time talking about training the younger people for the transfer of power. But how much time do we spend thinking about and preparing the

Decide how to manage consolidation, nontraditional funding sources, and the growing family tree.

generation that is giving up power? We have to devote time to training them, to helping them understand that there is life after the business. This will continue to be one of the major challenges facing family business owners.

The fifth and last challenge is one inherent in older businesses such as the Mennen Co.—the growing family tree.

In my generation, we have four branches of the family and a total of 14 members. Anyone who has sat in a meeting with all of us quickly realizes that, on any given subject, there are many different opinions. In the fifth generation, we have 22 family members. The tree is growing wider and sprouting many divergent interests. Some of the personal wishes are in conflict with the business wishes.

This is a process that takes time. It takes communication. Most of all, it takes trust. One of the biggest issues is how a family member who is neither in management nor on the board can have a say in the company. How does a family member who feels that the company should reinvest less and pay out more to stockholders, or who believes that a proposed product may be environmentally unsound, make his or her opinion heard? And if you are an in-law, where can you express a viewpoint that you feel strongly about?

To make sure that family members not directly involved in the business have a voice, each branch had appointed a representative to speak for the members' interests. The four representatives met periodically, and, if they agreed that a major point should be raised with the company, they would take it before the board. But again, this process can work only if there is trust—trust, for example, that each representative will speak out forcefully for the views of his siblings and their spouses, as well as for his own views.

Let me end by telling you about our fifth generation, which ranges in age from 8 months to 25 years old. They're dynamite, and we're sure that other companies are going to think so, too. When they enter the job market, they are going to get attractive offers. In the past we had to compete for their talents. We had a program to introduce them to the Mennen Co., to show them what kind of opportunities it could offer. One of the major elements of this program was a summer weekend seminar to teach them about business, and about life in general. Summer employment was another part of the program. We couldn't expect that 113 years of tradition and hearing about the many satisfactions of working in a family enterprise were sufficient to bind them to us. And you shouldn't either.

— *G. Jeff Mennen*

Team-Building and Consensus

Creating agreement and empowerment

To foster cooperation at the top, your group must agree on goals, the kind of leadership they want, and ground rules by which to operate.

WE OFTEN HEAR IT: In any business, someone has to be in charge. Particularly in a family enterprise with many active members—parents, brothers and sisters, cousins—it has to be clear who has the final say.

In some family firms, no one is in charge. Fearing a loss of family harmony, the parents avoid selecting a child to lead the company in the next generation. This nonsolution only intensifies the competition between siblings and creates confusion throughout the company.

In other companies, however, someone may be too much in charge. Typically in a patriarchal family business, the father sees to it that the stock is divided equally among his children, then tells the oldest male: "Son, when I am gone, it is your job to take care of things." Patriarch Jr. then has a dilemma: While dad may want him to be in charge, some of the other children certainly don't. He may begin to feel that his siblings are constantly critical of him, and that they don't appreciate the burden he bears. So he will stop communicating with them and do things only his way.

That kind of leadership, of course, can create resentment and result in a lack of cooperation. In the long run, families can keep the peace and insure business survival only by building a consensus on how they will make decisions and who will take the lead. To do that, the members must consciously move beyond childhood rivalries and develop, step by step, a mature family community.

What are the practical steps to clarifying and empowering leadership? For most families, the first decision requir-ing consensus should be on how decisions will be made. The group must agree to hold a series of meetings to try to reach agreement on the goals of the family enterprise, to define the kind of leadership they want, and to establish some ground rules by which they will operate. They might agree to start with issues on which they can easily achieve a consensus and work up to more difficult issues.

Early in the process, the family has to resolve basic leadership issues: What kind of leadership, who will choose the leader, what kind of support can be given, and how management will be held accountable? Likewise, the leaders have to ask themselves: Am I prepared to operate under new ground rules? How can I best communicate what is happening in the business to other family members in order to strengthen the consensus?

Many family business leaders have deep fears about opening up greater family participation. They are concerned about losing control, and see dangers in giving voice to potentially obstructionist elements.

If they don't do it, however, they may eventually face a split in ownership. When hostility mounts in the family, the disenfranchised members typically force a buy-out or sale of the company.

A board of directors can play a useful role in helping the business leader overcome his fears. Outsiders who are brought into the consensus-building process take time to understand the issues and avoid "shooting from the hip." The family as a whole must establish its own order and discipline to prevent "troublemakers" from disrupting the process.

Establishing clear lines of authority and building a consensus is difficult in a family business when underlying emotional forces are in conflict. These forces become particularly intense when there are power struggles between generations or between siblings.

For example, the founder's need for absolute authority will often lead to battles with a son or daughter over issues of control. Sibling rivalry is, of course, a major barrier. A sister, for example, may be the brightest, most knowledgeable, and diligent of her siblings, but an older brother may find it hard to acknowledge her superior qualities. To accept a leader is to entrust one's interests to another, to give that person power over you in the specific context of the business. Many siblings who are on their way of becoming adults don't yet have enough self-esteem or feel secure about their own identity, and cannot willingly cede authority to a brother or sister.

To build a mature family community, family members have to realize the importance of preventing these issues from intruding on the business. A clear distinction must be made between family and business relationships.

Keeping the two types of relationships separate, and learning how to act in a way that is appropriate to each, is critical to the success of a family business. But it's hard to do, particularly when it comes to issues of authority and accountability.

When older emotional issues can be set aside, the family's natural leaders can perhaps emerge more easily. Landmark studies have described the qualities that elevate the chosen few to positions of authority. Of course, some rule by being formally or legally anointed: They have been chosen by a board of directors, or, given 51 percent of the stock. But others attract followers naturally, by their presence and style—that intangible "charisma."

A second source of authority is the respect that comes from "paying one's dues," from learning the business from the ground up an working hard along the way. A third source is plain likability; people will take orders more readily from a leader with whom they feel comfortable. A fourth, obvious source is competence. To gain authority, and maintain it, leaders must produce results that benefit the firm; they also have to have the guts to make the hard decisions.

Beyond competence and guts is vision. The ability to formulate and communicate an inspiring idea of where the business is going, and what it can achieve, is essential to any business enterprise.

In choosing a leader, families should look for all, or some combination of, these qualities. The success of the enterprise, however, can never depend upon one person. The business can rise to new heights only with consensus on values, and through cooperative effort. The family community is built on respect for each member's uniqueness, on support for each member's growth into a mature adult. By building a consensus, the family moves from paternalism and emotional immaturity to a sense of participation, ownership, and commitment to the business. Everyone has a voice; everyone's opinion is important; no one will be frozen out. And key decisions are made by consensus.

That kind of mature family community will surely get the leaders they deserve, the very best leaders.

— *Peter Davis*

The spirit of consensus

The Quakers have perhaps studied what it takes to achieve consensus more deeply than any other group. Here is a list of fundamentals on "What Builds Consensus" from the Quakers' Pendle Hill Center for Study and Contemplation in Wallingford, Pennsylvania:

1. An understanding of, and unity with, the ideals of the organization which make consensus rather than majority rule preferable.

2. An understanding of the individuals constituting the group and their idiosyncrasies.

3. A deep commitment to listening.

4. A clear sense of trust in the validity, even the divine validity, of each member's contribution.

5. An openness to learn from those who may be better informed in an area of particular concern.

6. An acceptance of the fact that individual knowledge untempered by group wisdom is often very shallow.

7. A willingness to deeply examine one's self, in particular, when a compromise between one's own point of view and that of the group could lead to consensus.

8. A commitment not to compromise when the matter at hand involves a moral issue that appears to be in conflict with one's understanding of one's own moral code.

9. A commitment to search actively and openly with other group members for clarity.

10. The deep belief that earnestly laboring for moral clarity through the consensus process often results in profound leaps of personal growth.

11. A commitment not to view each issue before the group as having the potential to change the course of human events, but rather to maintain perspective.

12. A commitment to actively support a consensus decision.

Building a cohesive management team

First, make sure the time is right. Then choose the right people and take actions so the team will run itself.

IN EVERY FIRST-GENERATION OF FAMILY BUSINESS there comes a critical point when the owner-operator has to acknowledge the need for a management team. The business can no longer be run by one or two people at the top. Instead, the founder has to learn to rely more on colleagues, both family and nonfamily; he has to trust them and hold them accountable.

A growing business still needs centralized, direction-setting leadership. But wise leaders recognize that success often depends on the energies and ideas of others. A balance has to be achieved between participative management and entrepreneurial management.

For a one-man band to become an orchestra leader requires a leap of trust. Family businesses have a real edge here. The leap of trust can be easier if it's to blood.

In his book *Innovation and Entrepreneurship*, Peter Drucker says that when the time has come to adopt team leadership, the owner must then address three questions:

1. Is the company at the turnover point? Management experts say that for a manufacturing company, the rule of thumb is $5 million to $8 million in sales and more than 125 employees. The process of shifting gears in management style should begin earlier, however—when the number of employees reaches 50 to 75. The turnover point occurs much sooner in the growth of service companies.

Another way to determine whether your business has reached that point is to measure its growing pains. Do your people spend too much time putting out fires? Are many people not aware of what others are doing?

2. What am I good at? Which of the company's needs could I meet with distinction? Even entrepreneurs who are willing to give up some control struggle with the question of what their new role will be. To be successful in delegating, the owner-manager has to have a clear idea of what his or her role will be.

3. What do I really want to do and believe in doing? Is this something the company really needs? An inventor-entrepreneur may wish to focus on R & D and let others manage. A sales-marketing genius may choose to concentrate on developing a marketing plan and extending

Throughout the process, take time to celebrate the good news. It builds confidence.

the company's sales territories. The founder should remain in charge of at least one key activity that he excels in and that the company needs.

Even more important, the owner must remain responsible for articulating a vision for the business. Vision is essential to building a management team—it is the team's inspiration and main energy source.

The danger is that the vision may get lost or damaged in the leadership change from one generation to another. Unless the family has a shared commitment to goals larger than its own ambitions, the management team may easily implode because of family arguments and power plays. The vision should put into words what everyone intuitively knows is the right path for the company. When others in the business hear it, they should go "Aha!"

Once set by the founder, the vision has to be sold and nurtured. Inside the business, it is fostered by one-on-one dialogues with each employee. Within the family, it's fostered by an ongoing discussion of values. The family team should ask themselves questions such as: "Have we stayed true to our family's original vision of the business? Have we improved on it, kept it current? If we walked out on the floor and asked an employee about the company's mission, what would the employee say?"

The next step in building a team is to get the right people in the right places. In a family business, this is likely to require some tough, objective decisions. How does one find the courage to tell a brother that he's not cut out to head sales? What argument will convince your oldest son that he's better off as second in command?

The team has to address questions like: What skills are essential to the company's success? What strengths are represented on our team? Where are the gaps? What is our plan for filling them in?

Forget about job descriptions for awhile. Give each member of the team honest, respectful feedback on how you see his or her special talents and weaknesses. Based on your discussion, create the best niche in the business for each person. Then go back and write job descriptions that formalize each position.

Many family businesses have good department heads on their management team. Fewer of them have management teams that work together across functions and that consistently put the company's overall objectives ahead of their departmental goals. In working with teams, there are four things to stress:

1. Team-building is a process, not an event. It can take several years for a team to come together.

2. Spend time on key relationships. Get in the habit of thinking and talking about relationships on the team. Have regular, ongoing discussions of how you work together.

3. Be ready to openly discuss conflicts and ways of resolving them. Nothing destroys a team faster than an unwillingness to bring disagreements and bruised feelings to the surface and discuss them. One of the best investments of time a team can make is on developing a common language and skill for conflict management.

4. Learn to manage big egos. Any entrepreneurial firm has at least one and often several. The trick is to become an active proponent of each person's particular genius.

Once such people see you are on their side and are a champion of their talents, you will have more leverage to confront them with the downside of their expansive character.

Throughout the process of team-building, take time to celebrate good news. The entrepreneur has a built-in warning device against any temptation to relax. But teams gain confidence from celebrating victories: It is one of the most powerful and least expensive ways to maintain morale and build a strong culture of cooperation. Stories honoring the team come out of these celebrations— stories that carry the vision of the family business forward faster than any other means.

— *Lila A. Lewey & Stephen B. Swartz*

Differences Between Generations

Advice from a founder to his son

One of the best examples of an owner's advice to his successor was penned in 1945 by Martin L. Davey Sr., president of the Davey Tree Expert Co. based in Kent, Ohio. His business philosophy contains good old-fashioned advice for sons—or daughters—assuming positions of responsibility in a family business today. For Martin Jr., the letter was a poignant legacy: His father died three months after writing it.

MY SON, now that you have returned from Army Service, it is my desire that you take over the active management of The Davey Tree Expert Company, with whatever help and advice you need from me... I hope you will take to heart the following advice because, my son, there is no substitute for experience.

Above everything, make your word good. But, be very careful about the promises you make. Take time to get the facts, weigh each matter carefully on its merits, then when you make a commitment, keep your word—under all possible circumstances and at whatever cost. If you ever find that it is impossible to keep a promise, for perfectly valid reasons or because of things beyond your control, then don't delay; tell the other person promptly and frankly.

Next, I would say, is to think of your clients before everything. They are your lifeblood. Make it your business to see that they get honest value, quality workmanship, and diligent, conscientious service. They will continue to pay a fair price for that kind of service, sufficient to yield a moderate profit with proper management.

Nearly all of our clients are good people. Therefore, if a client makes a complaint, see that it is promptly and fairly investigated, for the purpose of equitable adjustment. It is very rare that one of our clients has ever tried to chisel or defraud us. In such unusual cases, make him pay, and never serve him again.

You can't make good men out of poor ones. I tried it many years ago, and it simply will not work. If a man is lazy, let him go. If he is careless and indifferent, let him go. If he is dishonest, let him go. It follows, quite naturally, that you have left only men who are diligent, careful, interested, and honest.

Treat your employees as human beings. Good men are ambitious, frugal, and trustworthy. Therefore, you should reward the better men as they earn it, when and as they prove themselves, and before they have to ask for it. Be on your guard against the men who recommend themselves too loudly and aggressively. Some of the best men are a little too modest to push themselves forward. It is part of your job to find that kind and reward them.

I have always felt that good sales representatives should make good money, and have always been happy to see them do so. Make sure, however, that they deliver the kind and quality of Davey service that represents true Davey standards, principles, and ethics. No matter how good the thing is which you produce, you must sell it or go out of business. It goes without saying that the thing which the salesman sells must be really good or he is soon out of employment.

Watch your credit with a jealous eye, every phase of it. Don't ever let a note become overdue, unless there is no way to prevent it. Pay your notes on time. Make it one of the first orders of your business life to protect your credit, pay your bills, and have enough money in the bank to meet payrolls and all other proper and necessary business expenses.

This brings me to the next thing of great and equal importance. Watch expenses like a hawk. Question every expense that is not clearly necessary and wise. Bore into these things with determination. Never hesitate to order an unnecessary expense eliminated and see that it is done.

Any money that is wasted must come from the clients or the employees or the stockholders. One of your most important jobs is to say "No," and make it stick.

There is an old saying, "When in doubt do nothing." There is some merit in it. Many a time I have waited to think things over, get more facts, and weigh the arguments pro and con, and by so doing have avoided some bad decisions. Please understand that a necessary part of your daily work will be to make decisions and I am not advising you to put them off. But don't make snap judgments.

I would advise and urge that you stay out of the banking business; that is, lending money to employees, unless it is unavoidable. There always have been and always will be many such requests. It is quite natural. Usually, it is neither wise nor necessary.

Never do anything while you are angry. It probably will be wrong. If you feel highly incensed by something, write it down on paper and thus get it out of your system—but put the paper in your desk or in your pocket for a few days, and then you will probably feel differently and do differently. I have made some mistakes by not doing this.

Pay a man everything that is coming to him. If he adds up his expenses incorrectly, it is your duty to make it right and pay him in full. Likewise, if a client pays more than his bill, send him the difference.

Don't do something merely because a competitor does it, or merely because some well-meaning friend or associate thinks it is a good idea. Of course, you should never be against it for that reason. It might or might not be a good thing. Judge everything strictly on its merit—calmly, judicially, and deliberately.

Please, please, do not try to be popular in your business dealings. You simply can't manage a business properly and be popular with everyone. Some people are inclined to slow down and take it easy; they need to be spurred into action. Some are inclined to chisel if they can get away with it; they need sharp discipline. Some few may become cocky or overbearing or impolite; they need to have their wings clipped and to be brought back to earth.

However, you should try to deserve respect. To achieve this desirable end, you should always be just and fair and reasonable, tolerant of minor human frailties. In the long run, the solid qualities of character and old-fashioned virtues are of far greater importance than brilliance or shrewdness.

Beware of flatterers. They have a cunning way of wasting your valuable time.

Work toward perfection. You will never reach it, but the business will be infinitely better.

Save your own time, and see that all others respect your time. It is extremely valuable. Parcel it out systematically among people and things according to the order of their importance to the business. Some people talk too much and others are a bit shy. Just take time to get all the essentials and then make your decision, or say you will think it over (preferably the latter) and end the interview, going promptly to the next most important thing.

Do not burden yourself with details. You must employ others for that. Know all you can about every phase of the business, but get your information from reliable people who handle the details. No man can manage a business wisely or efficiently unless he gets his head up off his desk part of the time and does some intensive and constructive thinking.

If you expect others to be diligent workers, you must be one yourself. Set an example.

You ought to be friendly in a moderate and reserved sort of way. I mean genuinely friendly. And always be polite to everyone. When you give orders, always say please. It costs nothing and makes the order easy to take. For many years, whenever I have sent orders by wire, I have always used the word please, even if it were necessary to pay for an extra word. Everyone with any sense will know it is an order just the same. The occasional dumbbell who thinks he can disobey because you say please, or who thinks you are soft for that reason, should be taken off the payroll.

There is one thing about business that is crystal clear: You can never coast down hill. There never comes a time when you can sit back, blandly and comfortably, and feel that your work is done, that all your problems are solved for a considerable period into the future. There will likely be fewer serious problems, however, if you are diligent, watchful, and active every day. A successful business is like a well-made and well-oiled vehicle that travels steadily upgrade.

In all my experience in business and in public life, the rarest types of minds I have encountered are the judicial and the creative. The judicial mind, how rare that is! So many of us are the victims of our likes and our dislikes, our prejudices, our preconceived notions, and our own peculiar idiosyncrasies. If someone whom we dislike suggests something, we are against it. The judicial mind discards its own likes and dislikes, and judges everything on the basis of pure facts and proven merit. Therefore, I would urge you strongly to strive always to be judicial in your thinking about all things.

It is well to work earnestly toward perfection. You will never reach it, of course, in this imperfect world, but if you keep striving for it, persistently, your business will be infinitely better. The natural pull of human inertia and indifference is downward. Good management must pull steadily the other way. Never let success spoil you. I do not think it would, but these thoughts are a very ardent part of my philosophy. Keep yourself reasonably humble but self-reliant. Keep yourself natural and unspoiled. When difficulties or discouragements confront you, summon all your calm, determined moral courage, and keep going—forward.

Preparing the third generation

To ensure a successful transition to the third generation, the second generation must decide if it is running a "family-first" business or a "business-first" business. Then it must take steps to successfully launch the third generation on its way.

ONE OF THE MOST DIFFICULT TRANSITIONS that a family business must make is from the second to the third generation. It's not just that the third generation, accustomed to wealth and privilege, is likely to spend the business into bankruptcy. They also have a very difficult time getting their acts together and providing the leadership necessary for the business to survive.

In the third generation, there are typically many more family members who would like to work in the company. The cousins have grown up in different households and may have far different styles and points of view. There may be extremes of personality and huge disparities in competency as well as in financial need. There may also be lingering feelings of competitiveness or memories of past injustices carried over from the second generation.

The seeds for a successful transition to a third generation are sown early in the company's history. As he builds the business, the founder sets a tone for family involvement that is usually well established by the time his children take over. The tone in most businesses usually falls somewhere between two extremes: the family-first culture and the business-first culture.

In "family-first" businesses, family needs are primary. Business decisions that might generate family conflict are avoided. Members of the second generation are paid equally and share in all key decisions. Family ownership is zealously guarded and nonfamily managers tend to be regarded as "the help." If the company has a board of directors, it is likely to consist of family members who gather informally, perhaps with an attorney or accountant.

At the other extreme are "business-first" family businesses, which let children who want to work in it know that they must measure up to company norms and values that are above the needs of the family. The children may be told that they can't work in the business unless they are at least as good as professional managers, and that they will be paid for the job they do rather than who they are. In a business-first company, nonfamily managers have considerable power and influence. The company is likely to have a board of directors with people from outside the company on it that meets regularly in formal sessions.

The family-first businesses in the United States are common among certain ethnic groups—Jewish, Lebanese, Italian, Greek, Latin American—that give the family a central place. They tend to be small personalized businesses—like real estate concerns, jewelry stores, and restaurants—that depend for their success on the family's hard work and entrepreneurial energies.

By contrast, business-first companies are more often found in Calvinistic cultures that place a high value on institutions and the free enterprise system. The most successful large companies that are still family owned, such as Cargill and Bechtel, are all business-first companies.

The tilt toward one or the other end of this spectrum shapes the survivability of the business. In the family-first business, the kids in the second generation are set up as active partners. They trust one another, communicate easily on business matters, and generally have more drive and savvy than anyone they can recruit in the job market. Early on they get the message from parents that they must work together and resolve their conflicts.

Typically, the family-first enterprise is a brilliant success in the initial phase of second-generation management. The business is still growing and the excitement about that growth sustains the partnership. Mother may still be around to moderate any conflicts that arise. The spirit of "all for one and one for all" is so deeply ingrained that it would be embarrassing and painful for any of the partners to cut out of the business.

The difficulty with these partnerships is that it is hard to keep them alive once the glory days are over. After a honeymoon period, the partners enter a more realistic phase in which they may realize that one or more of their group has serious shortcomings. They may be stuck with a lazy brother or another who is a loudmouth. At about the same time, spouses may begin to assert themselves. As the in-laws insist on larger roles for the spouses in the business, they may drive a wedge between the partners.

In the next phase, the deficiencies have become ever

more real and aggravating. Disillusionment sets in. The partners spend much time apart from one another and have difficulties in coordinating their business activities. Their willingness to discuss and negotiate is limited. The partnership is held together more by the fear of an embarrassing breakup than by the desire to work as a team.

As the second generation's differences grow, the children now enter the picture and become an even greater force propelling the partnership toward breakdown. One partner can't stand his brother's son, who thinks he's a big-shot and doesn't have to work. Another resents having to train a partner's incompetent daughter. In some businesses, the partners can manage anything but the entry of the children into the business.

Besides their own differences, the third generation may bring with them the unresolved problems from the second. One partner may have felt that he was always treated as an inferior by his brother. As a result, his son may carry the grudge into the next generation and be overly aggressive on issues involving power and responsibility in the company. He says, in effect: "I'm not going to be treated like dirt, as my father was."

So in the worst of all possible worlds, the old partnership is dying just when the third-generation is struggling to build a foundation for their own working relationship. They can seldom work it out by themselves. Their parents get embroiled in their disputes and an intergenerational tug of war ensues. At that point, a large percentage of these businesses fall apart.

If family-first businesses are to survive, each generation must negotiate the terms of its partnership separately. The second generation must revitalize their partnership and reach the accommodations necessary to launch the third. Members of the third must reach their own understandings on decision-making authority, pay, and methods of resolving conflicts—but, again, that may not be possible unless their parents cooperate in planning succession.

In the business-first firm, the succession process is more reliable and more structured. The basic rules are put in place when the company moves from the first generation to the second. Ownership is separated from management. The board of directors participates along with family members in defining and developing the rules of passage.

Business-first companies may be somewhat more bureaucratic than other family businesses, but they are

How to treat your children at work

Dos and don'ts for parents who want to maintain a healthy relationship with their children at the office. "He" applies the same to "she."

Do treat your child like a grownup, which, in fact, he is.

Do behave toward your child with the same courtesy and attention that you would give to a non-related employee.

Do be clear in your instructions to your child. Just because you're related doesn't mean he'll automatically know what you are talking about. Let him know what you want, and make sure he knows when you're pleased with the way he has completed a task.

Don't meddle in your child's personal life, especially if he doesn't ask for advice about it. Set boundaries for yourself. Try to keep family problems at home, where they belong.

Do pay him what he's worth: not too much, not too little. Compensation should be set according to rates on the open market and not be a source of parental control.

Do give him a helping hand within the company. Try to have him report to someone who will not be threatened by his presence.

Don't allow competitive feelings to enter your relationship. The mere fact that your child is now old enough to work in the business means that you are approaching another stage of your life. The realization that he may some day replace you can be satisfying for a father, but it also can be painful. Try to accept this as the natural course of events.

Don't equivocate when it comes to planning for the future. Your child should know what to expect as he becomes more familiar with the business and capable of more responsibility. If a succession plan is not in the works, it should be. The same goes

for an estate plan.

Do hold your child accountable for results. When you introduce him into the company, you lose a certain amount of control over events. You should let him know that you welcome his fresh ideas on the problems and opportunities that he sees in the company. But your child must also learn that he will be held accountable for his performance, and for his behavior, which is a reflection of the company.

Do talk with your child, regularly and often. The most successful relationships have a history of good communication. Choose whatever format is natural for the two of you to "talk things over." Perhaps you could have lunch once a week, or take a walk, or drive to work together. Or you could schedule more formal, twice-a-week meetings during which you can talk about anything.

— *Marcy Syms*

more stable and usually do a better job of managing succession. The major challenge for these companies is dealing with the family problems that occur because of the priority given to business considerations.

Children who are not qualified to work in the company and are denied jobs will suffer from feelings of rejection. Even if they share in ownership, they may feel cheated. When the business is growing, any surplus may be reinvested in the company rather than distributed as dividends. Family members in the business have an opportunity to earn higher salaries as they company grows, which may create envy among those who do not work in it. Moreover, in a business that promotes people on merit, one sibling may be taking orders from another, even from a younger brother or sister.

The stresses created by these differences in status and wealth are justified only if the goals and traditions of the business seem worth it. If the family feels that perpetuation of the business is important for reasons other than money—to maintain jobs for loyal employees or to enhance the family's reputation and influence—they have an extra incentive for working out their difficulties. But if the business creates too much friction in the family, some members may choose the simpler way of securing their futures—selling their shares; or, if enough of them are fed up, they may sell the company.

According to one study, only about 10 percent of all family businesses will make it into a third generation. With the exception of a few types of smaller entrepreneurial businesses, those that succeed in making the leap usually adopt a business-first philosophy during the transition.

It is up to the second generation to see that a viable set of operating rules and procedures are worked out during the process for managing the company and employing family members. They must establish a board of directors to oversee the business according to agreed-upon criteria and codes of conduct. To maintain unity, they must see to it that all branches of the family feel they have an opportunity to participate fully.

Without a good plan and a clear goal to guide the family's participation, further success may be impossible—and some family members, faced with declining fortunes, may return to the founder's shirt-sleeve beginnings.

— *Peter Davis*

– II –

BUSINESS AND FAMILY

---◆---

MANAGING A BUSINESS is hard enough. Managing a family presents its own unique challenges. Executives in family businesses have to do both—simultaneously. Techniques for actively managing the business and the family's involvement in it are addressed in this section.

Good management begins with a common frame of reference for executives and employees: a credo, a constitution, a clear goal, adherence to certain values. These are covered in Chapter 4.

How to decide whom to hire from the family, and when, is the chief concern of Chapter 5. Maintaining family harmony and resolving conflicts—among family employees, and nonactive family shareholders—are addressed in Chapters 6 and 7. Co-management by sibling teams, a tough act to pull off, is covered in its own chapter.

Many times, conflict can be diffused with open and honest communication. Chapter 9 presents exercises for improving communication skills. To institutionalize good communication, more and more families are forming family councils. The result, as explained in Chapter 10, is greater family unity and greater business success.

Top executives can carefully manage all the family aspects of the business and still run into big trouble if they don't give nonfamily managers the respect, attention, and information they need to help the company prosper. Hiring the right outsiders, making them insiders, and keeping them fulfilled is the subject of Chapter 11.

Values and Mission Statements

A work constitution: respect and reward

Adopted by the family a century ago, The Mogi Family Constitution is a statement of values and code of behavior which was clearly designed to prevent family tension and instruct the young. Other families may learn from its gentle admonitions.

THE MOGI FAMILY of Japan started the Kikkoman Corp. as a local soy-sauce maker in the 17th century. Today it is an international company. The family now has eight branches, each of which is allowed to designate only one member per generation to work in the business.

Executive managing director Yuzaburo Mogi presented the Mogi Family Constitution at a recent conference. Adopted by the family a century ago, it is a statement of values and code of behavior which was clearly designed to prevent family tension and instruct the young. Other families may learn from its gentle admonitions.

1. All family members desire peace. Never fight, and always respect each other. Ensure progress in business and the perpetuity of family prosperity.

2. Loving God and Buddha is the source of all virtue. Keeping faith leads to a peaceful mind.

3. All family members should be polite to each other. If the master is not polite, the others will not follow. Sin is the result of being impolite. Families—young and old, master and workers—govern themselves by politeness; then peace will be brought of their own accord.

4. Virtue is the cause, fortune the effect. Never mistake the cause for the effect. Never judge people on whether they are rich or not.

5. Keep strict discipline. Demand diligence. Preserve order—young and old, master and workers.

6. Business depends on people. Do not make appointments or dismissals using personal prejudices. Put the right man in the right place. Loving men who do what they should bring peace to their minds.

7. Education of the children is our responsibility to the nation. Train the body and mind with moral, intellectual, and physical education.

8. Approach all living beings with love. Love is fundamental to human beings and the source of a life worth living. Words are the door to fortune and misfortune. A foul tongue hurts oneself and others. A kind tongue keeps everything peaceful. Be careful in every word you speak.

9. Keep humbleness and diligence, which have been handed down over the years from our forefathers. Make every effort to do as much as you can.

10. True earning comes from the labor of sweat. Speculation is not the best road to follow. Don't do business by taking advantage of another's weakness.

11. Competition is an important factor in progress, but avoid extreme or unreasonable competition. Strive to prosper together with the public.

12. Make success or failure clear, judge fairly punishment and reward. Never fail to reward good service, and don't allow a mistake to go unpunished.

13. Consult with family members when starting a new business. Never try to do anything alone. Always appreciate any profit made by your family.

14. Don't carelessly fall into debt. Don't recklessly be a guarantor of liability. Don't lend money with the purpose of gaining interest, because you are not a bank.

15. Save money from your earnings, and give to society as much as you can. But never ask for a reward nor think highly of yourself.

16. Don't decide important affairs by yourself. Always consult with the people concerned before making a decision. Then employees will have a positive attitude in their work.

A family credo: Love and honesty

For effective relationships, divide tasks, agree on growth, be honest, and instill a love of the business.

McSWAIN'S HANDMADE FURNITURE in Charlotte, North Carolina, is one of the region's last furniture companies to remain in the hands of its founding craftsman. Owner Eulan McSwain, wife Frances, and son Mike have kept their family and their business healthy by observing a few basic principles:

● Share responsibilities and divide tasks. The head of a business shouldn't try to assume all the roles. If he does, relatives will not be encouraged to come into the business or to stay, nor will the survival of the business be insured once the owner retires or dies.

● Not all businesses need to grow large and powerful. Some businesses may not be able to maintain quality if they grow too quickly or assume too much debt. Determine long-term objectives early on. Stick with them—but don't be afraid to be flexible.

● Instill a love of the business in relatives. Talk about the business at work and at home. Be honest about its pitfalls.

● Encourage scions to work first outside the firm to gain confidence and applicable skills. Family members will then have no regrets about not having worked elsewhere. They'll come back more qualified.

● Once family members come into the business, have non-family personnel help train them and critique their performance. Family owners can promise to be objective with relatives, but may find it difficult. Reward honesty and constructive criticism.

● At work treat family no differently from other employees. Criticize, praise, reject, and uphold decisions. Avoid slipping into parent-child roles at the office. Admit mistakes to each other. Humor and honesty are great levelers.

● Prove that the child will inherit the business, if qualified, by giving up power gradually rather than making vague promises that "Someday all this will be yours."

● Pursue other interests while young and healthy. As retirement approaches, it's usually too late to cultivate new interests. Consider hobbies, teaching, community service, a new business.

● Get outside expertise before a crisis strikes or before succession problems occur. No business is too small to set up some type of outside board or advisory council.

— Barbara B. Buchholz & Margaret Crane

Family firms prefer profit over growth

Family business owners often have quite different goals from those of the public companies, and make different use of management tools in reaching these goals. Here are some norms to judge by.

FAMILY BUSINESS OWNERS are more concerned with improving profitability and reducing debt than they are with growing their companies, according to a large, 1993 survey done of family business owners.

When asked to indicate what their most important goals were, 89 percent of the owners chose "Increased profitability" (see chart below). Ranking second, at 76 percent, was "Increasing the value of the business." The relatively low priority (37 percent) given to expanding the business indicates that owners "seem prepared to sacrifice growth in favor of preserving their financial health," according to François de Visscher, president of the financial consulting firm de Visscher & Co. and an advisor to the survey group.

The results also indicate that many family firms have an informal management approach (see chart on next page). Some advisors consider this problematical; only 42 percent of the owners surveyed have written business plans, and only 51 percent hold regular family meetings.

The survey queried owners of 614 family businesses with at least 10 employees and annual revenues in excess of $2 million. It was conducted for the Massachusetts Mutual Life Insurance Co., in Springfield, by the Gallup Organization, and was designed by Mathew Greenwald &

Very important financial goals

Increasing profitability of business
89%

Increasing value of business
76%

Providing access to capital for the business
64%

Reducing debt level of the business
63%

Increasing family's wealth independent of the business
51%

Expanding size of business
37%

Providing liquidity to shareholders
28%

Management tools used

Formal and regular employee review
59%

Set compensation plans
57%

Written employee manual
56%

Written job descriptions
53%

Regularly scheduled meetings with family
51%

Regular board meeting
42%

Written business plan
42%

Associates working with a panel of family business experts. Among the other findings:

- 24 percent of owners do not want to transfer the business to a relative.
- 74 percent of those who do intend to pass on the business to a relative do not have a written succession plan.
- 83 percent of those with more than 250 employees intend to pass on the business, but only 10 percent have a written succession plan.
- 30 percent have no trusted advisor outside the family.
- 40 percent have spouses who are involved in day-to-day operations.
- 21 percent consider cash flow their most important source of capital; another 63 percent consider it very important.

Perpetuating family values in the firm

Installing a performance management system will allow the company and employees to grow around the critical factors that make the family successful.

WHEN YOU OWN A BUSINESS, you'll do anything to keep the customers satisfied, and you try to convey the family business values to every employee. You have a simple and trustworthy feedback system: your eyes and ears, which can keep focused in a small operation.

But your eyes and ears cannot see and hear everything in a growing business. There are too many employees who did not intuitively understand the family's values. The family needs to create a system to insure not just that its values are espoused, but to see that they are practiced.

Family businesses do not necessarily have to cotton to strategies espoused by "professional" managers—those with degrees and formal training. You may need to hire new managers, but MBAs are trained to apply, not design, models to business problems. There is an alternative strategy, called the performance management system (PMS), which allows you to perpetuate the very characteristics that made the family business grow successfully.

The first step in any PMS is to observe what everyone is doing on their jobs, to identify the critical success factors for their position. At the same time, family members must figure out formally how their values are reflected successfully in their day-to-day actions: how they interact with customers, how they treat employees, the percentage of time they spend with customers compared with the time they spend on administrative tasks. Then you must identify gaps between the family's values and everyone's actions. To bridge any gaps, you should determine and set numerical standards for each worker's and manager's critical success factors—the amount of repeat business, employee turnover, or customer satisfaction you expect. Last, you must create an ongoing feedback system that will provide reliable information about how each store, department, division, and person is performing against the new criteria.

There are several ways to make sure that people are living up to your values. For instance, you can set up an ongoing customer survey index based on the standards the business enjoyed during some past ideal period before growth began to crimp your style. You can conduct interviews of customers as they enter the store, as they leave, or use phone numbers on charge receipts to call customers. Employees and managers in each unit should keep a weekly list of customer complaints and comments, and compare their record to the overall store or department's standing. They should monitor returned merchandise, repeat business, and other variables—their critical success factors—to measure their own performance objectively.

Everyone fills out a one-page report that lists actual, versus expected, results for critical success factors. This is a great substitute for the dreaded, run-of-the-mill performance evaluation. In the traditional performance review system, a manager sits down once a year, maybe twice, and tells subordinates whether they are producing enough widgets, meeting quality standards, and displaying a positive enough attitude. This retrospective process is passive and rigid, allowing no ongoing improvement.

The PMS is responsive to problems that may underlie eroding performance. Every week when employees report how well they are meeting goals, their manager has an opportunity to emphasize how closely their performance is aligned with the family's values. For instance, a worker may proudly submit a report that shows she is producing 10 percent more widgets than last week. If the family business is more concerned about quality than quantity, her manager can point out that she should slow down, or perhaps take a course on a new software system that will enable her to meet the goals the company truly cares about.

Also, workers who track their performance weekly are more likely to think of creative ways of removing obstacles. A worker who has to report a slip in quality one week may suggest that a new wrench would let him adjust a machine himself instead of waiting for maintenance.

The PMS reinforces the company's values and helps workers solve ongoing problems. It also lowers training costs (because you know exactly where to focus training dollars), and enhances job and personal satisfaction.

A retail chain with $6 million in sales recently put together a PMS after its three family owners realized their six stores had outgrown their management capabilities. The symptoms included high turnover among the 50 nonfamily managers and employees, a drop in repeat customers, and the erosion of profits. The owners were way out of touch with their expanding empire. They thought they were doing everything right. They hired a cadre of managers to computerize accounting and inventory systems, and to design a formal structure for the stores. The computers were doing their job, so the owners figured the mangers must not be doing theirs.

The family members were convinced they were the only ones who could run the business; there simply were not enough of them to go around. Indeed, the family's style had worked well when there were only three stores: one member ran each site. But they expected their high-priced hired guns to duplicate the family's style and strategies and to help them manage the company precisely the way they would.

The owners were unknowingly not communicating what they wanted from their managers. How did they clear up the confusion? They set precise goals for everyone at every level.

A sample of critical success factors for the owner included:

Operations: He will visit each store three times a week to observe operations and talk to the people there.

Personal strategy: He will review all performance management programs weekly and set objectives for himself based on those reports.

Business strategy: At least one day a week he will review longer-term goals in the areas of profit-making, staffing, meetings, operations, and new directions for the business.

Feedback: Store clerks will monitor customer complaints attributable to their department; repeat business; the ratio of number of customers served to number of units sold.

As the family learned, a company doesn't have to compromise its unique and personal culture of growth. But at some point, the family culture will not run on automatic pilot. That doesn't mean it's time to turn over the keys to armies of MBAs. It means it's time to dissect, define, and communicate the family's strong and successful values. Everything from job descriptions to financial accounting must concentrate on preserving the unique ingredients that made the family business successful.

— *Jeffrey S. Davis*

> *The family culture will not run on automatic pilot. You must take action to preserve it.*

Employing Relatives

The pros and cons of nepotism

Family business owners are always concerned that the employment of relatives can affect the morale of employees and the company's ability to attract top executives. Thirty years ago the Harvard Business Review *studied corporate attitudes toward nepotism in one of the most comprehensive, in-depth explorations ever done on the topic. The 1965 survey covered 2,700 leaders of public and private companies nationwide. The results provide a great deal of practical advice on the hiring and supervision of family members, and how companies can use nepotism to their advantage. The* Review *summed up that advice in a Jan.-Feb. 1965 article, excerpted below.*

FIRST COMES THE QUESTION of how to decide whether or not to employ a manager's relative. The study has produced a variety of ideas on the subject:

Do have a group of the company's executives not related to him pass on his qualifications. In companies where nepotism occurs very often, fairly often, or occasionally, there is strong agreement with the wisdom of this procedure; nearly seven of every ten respondents consistently favor it.

Do consider the possibility of staying out of the question yourself if you are a senior relative—but don't feel obliged to abstain. The decision to hire, say 37 percent of those who have been related to other managers, should be made by executives who are not related to the candidate. Many of the respondents emphasized the strength of their convictions with extra written comments.

If the senior relative does decide to participate in the hiring decision, his main problem is how to deal with his bias. Some executives warn him about being too partial. Others warn him against expecting too much of a relative and hence being too "hard" on him.

Do consider the possibility that a would-be nepot may profit from two or more years of experience in another company before joining an organization where he has family ties. Such experience would be made a requirement by 58 percent of those from companies where nepotism occurs very often. Among those who have personally been nepots or patrons [senior executives related to nepots], there is 54 percent agreement with the wisdom of such a requirement.

Do consider the advisability of the nepot's obtaining some kind of formal business training or preparation before he goes into administrative work with relatives. A degree from a business school is favored by 38 percent of those who have been nepots or patrons. A popular requirement is one to three years of apprenticeship in factory work, field selling, and/or clerical work; 58 percent of nepots and patrons consider this desirable.

Don't turn the hiring decision over to outsiders, however skilled they may be in executive recruiting. Approximately seven respondents in every eight show lack of enthusiasm for delegating the hiring job to consultants.

Don't employ a relative who does not have one or more highly "visible" assets—at least, if there is much possibility of resentment or misunderstanding among nonrelatives in the company. Respondents have varied opinions as to what this asset should be, but the advantage of some "strong point" is mentioned repeatedly. Some think it should be demonstrated managerial capacity. Others think it should be exceptional intellect or personality. Still others think it should be know-how.

What about the training and supervision a nepot receives after being hired?

Do have him take intensive in-company training, say 67 percent of businessmen from companies where nepotism occurs very often.

Do consider the possibility of extensive but informal on-the-job coaching for the nepot from his superiors, say nearly two-fifths of the respondents from companies where nepotism occurs often. The fact that a majority do not urge such training would indicate, however, that this step is far from mandatory, in their opinion.

Don't let the nepot work under the senior relative's supervision, say 64 percent of nepots and patrons, and even more—73 percent—of others. But there is not such strong agreement that the nepot should be forbidden from working in the senior relative's department or division, so long as he is not under the latter's direct supervision.

Don't let the junior relative come into the company unprepared for the undercurrents and backlash his appointment may create. The pros and cons of nepotism should be thoroughly explained to him, and a course in human relations for him is a must. He should also be asked this question: "Are you prepared to understand nepotism in all of its disadvantages, and will you be sincere in trying to hold the detrimental factors in check?"

Finally, what suggestions do our executives have for policies concerning nepotism?

Do consider the possibility of adopting specific, written statements of management's policy toward nepotism, say a great many businessmen from companies employing relatives in management. The fact that about half do not check this step as desirable, however, suggests that nepotism is too "touchy" a topic in many organizations to be committed to writing.

Do announce that management is committed to the standard of objectivity (even it if has no formulas or devices for assuring it). Urgings of this kind are repeated over and over in the questionnaires. The commitment should be communicated to all managers. It should also be communicated at the start to the junior relative. Make it coldly plain to him that he gets and holds the job on the basis of his own qualifications and productive perfor-

Obstacles for the nepot

Managers responding to the *Harvard Business Review* study noted that a nepot, once hired, might face attitudes or self-perceptions that could add difficulty to his ability to perform his job.

One problem in particular had been observed much more than others: that the nepot finds it difficult to work productively with others and earn their respect… because others tend to suspect his authority was not earned (even if in fact it was). Respondents also indicated that management might tend to think the relative of an important executive will take it easy because he feels protected.

Some respondents worried that the pressure to live up to others' expectations would inhibit the nepot's self-development. They also feared that a nepot would come to doubt his ability to succeed without the patron's help. Quite a few worried about the nepot's self-esteem, the image he presents to others, and difficulties of self-evaluation. "He'll never know," wrote one market research manager, "if he's worth half his salary or twice the amount."

mance. Also, the relative should be measured against able nonrelatives. He should be put to competitive tests, where the ability of one person is bound to outshine the ability of others. Not written tests, but instances that will indicate one's character, morality, sense of justice, business acumen, and so forth.

Don't go along with any proposals that the number

Family employees: Good points and bad

The 2,700 people responding to the Harvard Business Review *study were asked to indicate the greatest advantages and disadvantages of nepotism. They are ranked below, from greatest to least important.*

Advantages

1. Compared with nonrelatives, a relative is likely to feel a stronger sense of public responsibility in his work.

2. A relative is likely to fit in better than nonrelatives.

3. A relative is likely to take more interest in the company than do nonrelatives.

4. When an executive's relative is employed in management and proves to be capable, the morale of the management team is stimulated.

5. Compared with nonrelatives, a relative of an executive is likely to be more loyal and dependable.

6. Relatives in management help to assure continuity and effective carry-on of corporate policies.

7. Because an executive's relative in a junior position does not have to "play up to the boss," he can set his own pace and develop his potentials better.

Disadvantages

1. Nepotism tends to create jealousy and resentment among the employees.

2. Nepotism tends to discourage outsiders from seeking work in the company.

3. If a relative is hired as an executive and proves to be inadequate, he cannot be fired or demoted as readily as others can.

4. It is impossible for managers to be objective about the qualifications of their own or other managers' relatives.

5. In management groups where relatives are influential, family interests tend to be put ahead of corporate interests.

6. Nepotism may cause loss of respect for the intelligent judgment, integrity, and objectivity of top management.

of relatives in management be limited to an arbitrary figure or percentage of total employees, say most respondents.

Don't set the salary range for relatives lower than for nonrelatives in comparable positions, say the great majority of executives from companies with or without nepotism. Only one or two in a hundred see any wisdom in this kind of salary discrimination.

— *David W. Ewing*

Rules for hiring family

Some owners set strict requirements for relatives who want to join the business, others don't. But all have definite ideas about the level of education and experience newcomers should possess.

F EW FAMILY BUSINESS OWNERS are tougher on their own kind than the men who run Coors Brewing Co. in Golden, Colorado. Bill Coors, grandson of the founder, and his nephew Pete govern the hiring of family members with a traditional principle: Give them a job at the bottom and make them work their way up.

Bill, chairman of the parent company, and Pete, chairman of subsidiary Coors Brewing, add that specialized training is the key for any family member who wants to succeed. Pete and his brothers have engineering degrees, which Bill says is the technical basis for holding down a job at Coors. Pete has an MBA on top of that.

Family members with standard business degrees or other general educational backgrounds can expect to be asked to go back to school to get training in an appropriate specialty.

In a first-generation business, it's usually Mom and Dad who decide what requirements, if any, should be set before the kids can join the company—and, when the children show up for work, what explanation, if any, is owing to the other employees. Customarily, those parents who want to make certain their children have minimal qualifications will insist that they get at least a college degree and perhaps some experience outside the business first.

In a fourth-generation company such as Coors, however, the matter becomes vastly more complicated. For older and larger companies, standards must be set to avoid the impression of unfairness and rampant nepotism. More specialized training is needed before family members can measure up to other employees. Generally, the family has grown, too. It may have several competing branches, with parents and their offspring, cousins,

spouses, and in-laws all vying for the top positions.

Family businesses tend to develop formal guidelines for the hiring of relatives when they have grown to a certain size, which varies according to the industry and the number of family members aspiring to join the firm. Very large companies, however, tend to avoid separate rules for family members and insist that, like other job candidates, they go through standard application procedures.

Several factors influence the necessity of this approach. Separate standards send the wrong message to other employees—even if qualifications are tougher. Special handling also undermines the authority of hiring personnel.

Family firms take varying approaches to the hiring of kin, depending on their stage of evolution. Some families write down specific requirements. Others establish a philosophy in a family charter. Many others still have no formal rules but continue to rely on gut appraisal of the candidates and their talents.

And yet there are several common themes that emerge from talking to a number of families. Many agree, for example, that young people graduating from college clearly benefit from working at another company before joining the family business, even those who are being groomed as successors from their early days. It establishes a feeling of self-worth. It's critical that young people accomplish things at a company where their name doesn't carry any weight. It also enables them to make their first mistakes elsewhere.

Nowadays some level of higher education is a common requirement in many family companies. Gone are the days when the kids started working at the office right out of high school. Additional schooling is now viewed as fundamental to making it in today's competitive world. It's also a necessary step for anyone who wants to distinguish himself as being capable of management.

Specialized training is fast becoming a key qualification, as families appreciate the value of professional management. More and more owners prefer to see children get degrees that are specific to the position they expect to shoot for once they join the firm.

A brother, trained as an accountant, can become CFO. A stepfather with a background in finance could be head of stockholder relations. And a stepbrother who was a lieutenant colonel in the Air Force would qualify as head of operations.

Written rules seem to evolve as companies get bigger and older. Most family businesses start out making hiring decisions on a case-by-case basis, says Gerald Le Van, an attorney and president of the Family Business Foundation in Baton Rouge, Louisiana. But it's never too soon to make rules. Most families just don't get around to it until they're confronted with a tough case.

At medium-size companies, family owners tend to have some kind of written requirements or statements of guidance. To ensure objectivity—or for the sake of appearance —they often leave the final decision to a board of directors, a family council, or a senior non-family manager.

Once drafted, the rules are presumed to apply to all relatives, whether direct descendants, distant cousins, or in-laws. An emerging trend for families who desire graduate education, particularly MBAs, Le Van says, is to have college grads work for several years and then go back for the advanced degree. It gives young men and women some practical experience against which to apply the lessons they learn at school.

Some family leaders are also beginning to place minimum age requirements on the incoming generation, refusing to hire children until they reach, say, their late 20s or early 30s. These owners figure that people in their 20s need the hazard of getting fired, of getting transferred. They have to confront a sense of risk, of failure, before they mature enough to do a good job. This risk just isn't as great in the family firm.

All the rules in the world cannot mask the fact that hiring, at some point, becomes a subjective decision. There are many pluses to having family members on the corporate team—they are often more committed than nonfamily employees to helping the business succeed, they bring a certain cachet to customers who like to deal with "the people in charge," and they harbor a long-term view which often results in better decisions and more stable progress.

Still, rules help demystify the hiring process and protect the family firm from being besieged with unqualified relatives who only bring unnecessary tension. Better to have the family live by the rules, than have the family rule your life.

— *Mark Fischetti*

Do you even want to hire family?

Establishing rules or guidelines by which to hire family members creates a common understanding for everyone. But before you even draft rules, you'd be smart to consider whether you actually want any other family members in the business, advises W. Gibb Dyer Jr. of Brigham Young University, an expert on family business. Dyer suggests family members ask themselves the following questions before jumping to step two:

1. Do I trust other members of my family?

2. Do other members of my family generally share the same goals?

3. Is my family able to handle disagreements and conflicts?

4. Do family members share their feelings and concerns rather than keeping them to themselves?

5. Can I make decisions with (rather than for) family members?

6. Do family members have knowledge, skills, or experience that will help the business?

If you answer no to one or more of these questions, Dyer says, you had better develop a strategy to overcome the weakness. Otherwise, choose not to employ family members.

Preventing greed and animosity in the second generation

The first step is to prevent children from believing they are entitled. If it's too late, then corrective actions must be taken.

IN MANY BUSINESSES, the proliferation of stakeholders has threatened to destroy the company. If America has become a society of entitlements, as many have said, nowhere is that sense of entitlement more focused—or more destructive—than in the family business.

In one of the most common scenarios, family managers need money for continued growth, but non-participating shareholders—who for years milk the company for income while contributing zilch to its success—will not hear of it. This kind of business has a bunch of feisty, antagonistic, successor-generation shareholders who understand little about the business and feel they are getting cheated. Both family and nonfamily managers, who keep the business afloat, ask themselves: What can be done?

This sense of entitlement begins early, when kids are taught they have some God-given right to benefit from the business without concern for what they contribute. The message heard from too many parents is not, "Work hard to be accepted." Instead, the kids hear: "Whatever you get out of the business is your right."

There are several prescriptions for these matters. In choosing successors, the best guarantee that only the qualified will be considered is the existence of an operable board, with outsiders on it; in a meritocracy, someone has to be the judge.

Children who lack aptitude or commitment to the business should be encouraged to look for employment elsewhere. When siblings can't get along, when their rivalries persist into adulthood, you shouldn't bring them all into the business. You shouldn't give stock to children when they're juveniles just to save some tax money. Hostile spouses can be a powerfully divisive force; wait to see whom the children marry and whether or not their spouses can accommodate the needs of the family and the business.

Unfortunately, many owners do not confront these issues. They bring warring family members into the firm in hopes of teaching them to get along better. The business is expected to provide therapy rather than taking care of the economic well-being of the family.

Even when it becomes clear that kids in some families will never work as a team, their parents still search for a solution that will keep everyone "happy." Some owners try to create separate areas within the business so that siblings can have their own turf and never have to come in contact with their brothers and sisters and cousins. Wounds continue to fester beneath this Band-Aid, however; sooner or later, the blood-letting resumes, usually four cars back from the flowers at the funeral.

Some other owners prefer to believe that conflict in their family doesn't exist. They can be brought to their senses and mobilized to act rationally only when given a blunt warning: When they are gone, their grieving widow will be left to deal with the problems they ignored.

While a founder is alive and in the business, he may be able to keep warring siblings apart, through threats and promises. And sometimes after the father is gone, the peace is kept "for mother's sake." When both parents pass on, however, no one is around to prevent war from breaking out.

Siblings who cannot cooperate should be asked to leave. When dissident shareholders become disruptive, the only solution is to get rid of them, to "prune the tree." In the long run, buying them out is the cheapest way to solve the problem. The longer the owner waits, the more costly—and rougher—the solutions are for all concerned.

Natural leaders bring out leadership in others. They understand that responsibilities go along with rights. They are strong and secure enough to patiently explain their actions and get others to buy in. To them, succession is not the golf club memberships or company cars, but the opportunity to work hard for the glory of the enterprise and the welfare of all.

— *Léon Danco*

Maintaining Family Harmony

Making room for in-laws

Instead of ignoring them, encourage in-laws to explain their views about family behavior. You'll be surprised at what you learn. And keeping them in the dark only heightens the chances for controversy, anyway.

IN-LAWS bear the brunt of countless jokes aimed at their alleged incompetence or tendency to interfere. Family business spouses, though, can often help, instead of hinder, the family business.

Because they were raised in a different family, spouses don't tend to get caught up in the emotional eccentricities most families develop. In-laws, of course, are the products of their own family shtick, but that doesn't seem to detract from their ability to spot emotional undercurrents more objectively than members of the family they married into.

It's not unusual for family business members to resist involvement of the spouses initially. They fear that in-laws will unnecessarily complicate the issues at hand and cause a further split. On the contrary, experience has shown that when spouses do become involved, family business problems are solved more quickly and efficiently.

Therefore one ground rule is that in-laws should be allowed to attend and should participate in selected family business planning meetings. You don't have to invite them to help run the business, but allow them to sit in on discussions focused on the overlap between family and business.

The presence of spouses usually inspires the family members to be on better behavior; they are not so quick to act disrespectfully toward one another. Also, spouses are often the only people who, during heated arguments, can tap their husband or wife gently on the shoulder and say, "Honey, I don't think you are really hearing what your brother is saying."

Excluding in-laws outside the business can be downright dangerous. There is nothing worse than second-hand information, especially when it comes from someone emotionally involved in a conflict. When a family member comes home from the office and complains to her husband about what went on at the compensation meeting that day, her husband, reacting to a one-sided and somewhat distorted report of the event, will of course take his wife's side and fan the flames. He is likely to say, "My god, you let your brother get away with that?" Next day at the office, at his proddings, she will be doubly divisive.

The husband understandably takes his wife's side, because he loves her. But the belligerent advice he is bound to give her, in response to her distorted account, only ends up entrenching the entire family in resentment.

Of course, spouses can also complicate family business discussions with their own issues and emotional hot-buttons. Sometimes, for instance, spouses don't get along with each other, and create new problems. That's all the more reason to involve them. After all, avoiding their feelings and concerns does not make them disappear.

Including spouses requires an investment of time and

Keeping in-laws informed

There are pragmatic reasons for including in-laws in family business planning meetings...

They provide a dose of objectivity.

They tend to keep the family on its best behavior.

They can help their spouses clearly understand emotionally charged messages.

... and dangers in not doing so.

Information about decisions that affect them may be distorted.

Their own concerns and issues may never get resolved without the family business forum.

energy. But one way or another their concerns will surface. It's always a case of pay me now or pay me later. If it's later, you will usually wind up paying with interest, which will generally compound at the same rate at which family disharmony grows.

When spouses do participate, they always bring the positive benefit of their unique perspective. In the event they also bring issues or concerns to the meetings, it's still more efficient to deal with them directly and up front. Solving family business issues requires the cooperation and positive involvement of everyone affected, and spouses are a valuable source of good will for family owned business problem-solving.

— Tom Hubler

How to handle discontented kin

There are two options for unhappy family employees and shareholders: buy them out or give them a useful role, with a voice in decisions. The second option is often feared, but if done right, has a great deal to offer.

OVER TIME in family firms, it becomes harder and harder to keep everyone happy. Young family members who see little prospect of ever running the business think about leaving. Family stockholders in third-generation companies may get little in the way of dividends while the managers pay themselves well; they get more and more frustrated when they feel they have no influence.

When dissatisfaction grows, the response of the power structure in the business may be: "Be quiet and be grateful for what you have." Or, "Don't you realize how difficult it is to make money today! Don't you see what heroes we are in a very difficult business!"

Family businesses cannot afford to ignore expressions of discontent and dissent from their members. The leaders must establish forums in which the disenfranchised can have a voice, and, if they still want out, must make it easy for them to sell their stock. Otherwise, the pent-up dissatisfaction may one day explode.

A generation ago, a political economist named Alfred Hirschman wrote a landmark book about what people can do when the organizations they belong to no longer meet their needs. The title expresses the three options as Hirschman sees them: *Exit, Voice, and Loyalty.*

Some younger family members may finally choose the loyalty option, even though they are unhappy. They will declare loyalty to those who are running the show, hoping thereby to reap rewards that will ultimately compensate them for their feelings of deprivation. But the company's most appropriate responses should be to make exit easier and to develop a comprehensive but flexible set of voice options.

In a family business, exit is extraordinarily difficult. Often young family members feel they are stuck in their careers. These are people who should leave the business and go to work elsewhere, but for various reasons they are staying put. Perhaps after thinking it over, they are simply unwilling to give up their "golden handcuffs," for example, or they may feel they would be letting down their parents and siblings if they left.

If they want to sell their stock, they run into other, equally formidable barriers. Many families consider selling stock in the company to be an act of disloyalty, if not high treason. If you sell at the value that the family's lawyers have engineered for estate tax purposes, you should probably have your head examined. But if you insist on a higher price, the company may be forced to go into debt to buy you out; if the company goes down as a result, you are saddled with a lifetime of guilt. And if, in your greed, you force up estate taxes for everyone else, you and your lineage may be cursed for generations.

Shareholder liquidity is a fiction in most family companies, but it shouldn't be. Companies have much to gain by making exit easier. For one thing, letting young people sell out permits them to make career choices more in line with their true aspirations. For another, if all the kids are quitting, at least that lets the powers-that-be know they have to do more to keep the new generation interested.

Giving a larger voice to shareholders who are removed from the power structure is easier said than done—and one reason, of course, is that it threatens the power structure. The leaders may feel that the shareholders who complain the most are "chronic complainers" who are not really prepared to do the work necessary to be responsible participants.

In reality, this attitude often reflects myths and prejudices in family firms. There is the Pandora's Box myth: "Don't open that up, because you never know where it will lead us!" And there is the sleeping dogs myth: "Why bring that up to Aunt Tillie—it will only upset her." And there is the dumb-relatives routine: "Why confuse them with facts when they don't know the first thing about the business?"

Questions of participation go hand in hand with power issues. When the patriarch is alive, it's pretty clear where power lies. Once the patriarch is dead, family members may have a real fear of a loss of control. Differences over goals

Every Thursday at 4 p.m.

One patriarch of a well-known firm has made it a point to meet with young family members every Thursday at 4 p.m. without fail, no matter what. This man has built a billion-dollar company, but he always has time for his family. They appreciate it, and know their voices are being heard.

and objectives have to be openly discussed. If family members are unwilling to confront the issues, if they're reluctant to go to the mat with each other because it may break up the family, the business will be in danger of paralysis.

In a family business, the legitimacy of power is bestowed by the older generation, but also depends on the chosen leader's ability to continue meeting the family's needs and running the business according to family tradition. Encouraging participation is one way that the leader can maintain legitimacy in the eyes of other family members.

For the leaders the challenge is to increase participation in the business without losing control. That may take as long as half a generation and requires the family to re-examine issues of power and how it is used.

First and fundamentally, those in power must commit themselves to a process of real empowerment of the others. Convincing the leaders that it will be all right—that giving the kids some voice in decisions won't doom the company—requires persistence and tact.

Second, the family has to build a consensus in favor of including all the members and respecting their needs and opinions. Third, shareholders have to reach a consensus on some minimal ground rules for running the business—on growth targets, for example, or on the amount of risk that will be taken, perhaps even on payouts to shareholders.

Fourth, the family has to define the appropriate level of participation for each of the members. Too often, participation in family companies requires an all-or-nothing, lifetime commitment, like joining a church. Many young family members have a deep attachment to the business but don't want to dedicate their lives to it. There are supporting roles that they can play, for example: board member; family council member; board committee member; active shareholder (getting involved when important issues need to be resolved); family ambassador (showing up when a family presence is called for in the business or community).

To participate responsibly, family members may need some education in the business beyond what they have. Sometimes when we think of succession, we forget that there are two separate processes: succession in management and succession in ownership. Children who own stock but don't want to manage must be taught what they need to know to express themselves as owners. They have to learn something about the company, about management, about finance, and so on.

Finally, there must be forums for participation. The annual shareholders' meeting is seldom enough; perhaps the meetings ought to be semi-annual or quarterly. A board of directors that includes family members not active in the business may be more important to enhancing participation than to establishing management accountability (which it frequently doesn't do anyway).

Sometimes a new forum is necessary. Many families are establishing family councils, which meet in an informal setting and encourage all members to express their feelings freely. [See "Family Councils" later in this section].

Some have established auxiliary boards on which younger family members grapple with real issues and learn to function as board members.

Assuring family members that they will have voice in the company affairs, that their views will be taken seriously, calls for leadership. When the leaders are constantly bogged down in the day-to-day running of the company, they may neglect the process. But when leaders are responsive and show concern, half the battle is won.

— *Peter Davis*

Stock redemption for family owners

One of the keys to keeping the peace is providing ways for inactive shareholders to cash in their stock. Here's how to set up a stock redemption program that offers liquidity without hurting the company.

THE LACK OF LIQUIDITY options is the most frequently cited source of unhappiness among passive family shareholders. The demands of these shareholders frequently escalate in later generations at just about the time when larger family businesses have opportunities to expand or a need to diversify and require infusions of capital. At precisely the time when third- and fourth-generation shareholders are coalescing as a force to be reckoned with, management is resisting their demands for liquidity, setting the stage for family conflict. Under the emotional strain of being badgered for liquidity and constantly second-guessed, the managing shareholders often throw in the towel and sell the company, more out of frustration than rational choice. The collision of interests often damages family relationships irreparably.

All shareholders in family companies want a clear idea of what their investment is worth, how it compares with other, alternative investments, and how it can be liquified, if necessary. Succeeding generations are increasingly well educated and financially savvy. Aided by easy-to-use personal computers and portfolio-management software, they are likely to become more rather than less demanding of a competitive return on risk capital. Family businesses need a formal mechanism for valuing and liquifying privately held stock on a continuing basis, and intelligently factoring in the capital needs of the business so that conflicting claims for finite amounts of cash are minimized. The managers can also reap substantial benefits by establishing ongoing liquidity programs for stockholders who want to diversify their investments or get their hands on cash for personal uses.

Two types of programs can be used to provide ongoing liquidity: the annual redemption fund and the company-sponsored loan program. The most common of the two is the annual redemption fund, which allows shareholders to periodically sell their stock to other family members or, if they cannot find such buyers, to the company at a fixed, formula price. Under these programs, the company creates a pool of funds out of available cash flow in order to buy back stock during a predetermined period every year.

Funds for a company-sponsored loan program are provided by a different mechanism. The company arranges for a bank to loan money to its shareholders against their stock, usually at higher ratios of loan to stock value than a bank would normally offer borrowers. Under this arrangement, a company puts its credit behind that of its shareholders, in effect promising to make good on any loan in the event of a default—in which case it can reclaim the stock which is the collateral. The company-sponsored loan program is often used in combination with the annual redemption fund. The loan approach is particularly attractive to younger stockholders starting out in life, who may desire liquidity to fund new ventures or career education and yet may not want to sell stock in the family company for emotional reasons. The annual redemption fund is targeted more to the needs of older shareholders, who may want to diversify their investments or achieve liquidity for retirement.

Creative use of the redemption fund. A Midwestern family company faced a liquidity dilemma three years ago and solved it with an annual redemption fund. Founded in 1925, the company grew rapidly to become one of the largest auto parts distributors in its region. The company was led by four second-generation family members who

were active in management and a nine-person board that included highly respected outsiders. Although the company distributed established, brand-name parts and was reasonably profitable, it paid only modest and irregular dividends. Management was thus under increasing pressure to provide more liquidity from third-generation stockholders, members of the Baby Boom generation who were unhappy with their return.

To increase the long-term value of its stock, the company had diversified by investing in distribution outlets downstream and in real estate. But for many shareholders, the long holding periods common in real estate development were creating unacceptable risk-and-return trade-offs. A small but increasingly vocal group became convinced that the real estate values were in excess of the earnings value of the business and were clamoring for a sale of the business assets. In contrast, the active shareholders believed that the business was getting stronger through its captive distribution network. They also felt that the real estate assets had not yet matured to their full value. Management was therefore vehemently opposed to a sale.

To satisfy the dissidents, the company set up an annual redemption program tailored to the family's specific needs. The program approved by the board consisted of three parts. First, it set up a liquidity pool funded with annual contributions of 20 percent of cash flow. This pool is used to redeem shares of family members every year provided certain financial tests are met—for example, so long as the total book value of the company, as determined by the board, does not sink below a certain level and debt-to-capital ratios do not exceed a reasonably safe limit. Second, a formula was established to determine the price at which stock would be sold. The formula consisted of four measures: 1) pre-tax income, 2) earnings before depreciation, interest, and taxes, 3) book value of the company, and 4) after-tax market equity. Third, all transactions would have to take place within a limited time frame—45 days following the date that notices go out to shareholders. And, fourth, the price would be updated annually according to the formula.

Over a period of a few years, shareholders who sold their stock have received cash for personal use and for diversifying their investments, while buyers have increased their ownership in their preferred investment vehicle—the family business. By scheduling a fixed time period for such transactions, the company has maximized the opportunities to match buyers with sellers and thereby minimized the need to dip into the redemption fund. Meanwhile, management has been able to pursue longer-term projects as well as take advantage of short-term opportunities that might have been stymied by the dissidents. The recently developed distribution outlets, which had been opposed by some of the dissidents, have become large contributors to revenues and profits. The recovery in real estate values has enabled the company to complete a long-term mortgage financing. The company has thus realized some of the rewards of "patient capital."

There were also unexpected benefits from the program. The process of tracking stockholder value—by means of the annual formula price—provided shareholders with a better understanding of the macroeconomic and competitive pressures that influence stock values. Psychologically, the process helped to bind the loyalty of inactive shareholders to the family managers who were on the firing line. A new spirit of camaraderie developed between the "ins" and the "outs." In fact, when provided with a liquidity alternative and an unemotional framework for understanding value, many previously dissatisfied shareholders opted to retain their shares. The process drove home the point that they retain more wealth when the appreciation in value on the stock is unrealized than when they receive taxable cash dividends.

Management also learned some valuable lessons from the program. The emphasis on value exposed the inherent weakness in the cyclical auto parts business and persuaded the managers to invest in product and geographic diversification as well as in acquiring its own stores downstream. At the same time, board members became more conscious of the importance of maximizing shareholder value, which served to improve the company's strategic planning as well as its relations with shareholders.

Finally, the process of setting up the redemption fund improved communication with all shareholders and eased family tensions. The dissatisfied group felt that their concerns were finally being recognized and acted upon by management. By shifting more ownership to the shareholders who were most interested in the growth of the family business and preserving its heritage, moreover, the leaders also increased the prospect of a successful transfer of the company to the next generation.

Designing a redemption fund. The most critical step in designing an annual redemption fund program is to select a valuation methodology and funding mechanism that is tailored to the particular company and the dynamics of its industry. It is usually wise to engage experienced advisors to design the formula and reassure all shareholders of its objectivity and fairness.

Ongoing liquidity programs provide cash and ward off crises before they are reached.

The annual formula price is typically derived from standard valuation criteria, including income approaches, comparisons with values of comparable public firms, and data from previous arms-length sales. The formula differs slightly from standard valuation criteria, however, in its emphasis on available cash flow and borrowing capacity—since these are the primary sources of funds for stock redemptions.

The formula price and buyback fund must be responsive to changes in the operating business and the industry. For slower-growth, highly capital intensive industries, the most appropriate yardstick is often free cash flow, adjusted for annual capital investment. For high-growth industries, in contrast, after-tax earnings is frequently emphasized. Cash flow as measured by earnings before depreciation, interest, and taxes (EBDIT) is the most appropriate measure for industries such as broadcasting, communications, and food processing. Because of the operating leverage in their franchises or brand names, companies in these industries are often driven and valued by cash flow, for which EBDIT is an approximation.

The formula price allowed the managers of the auto parts supplier to demonstrate the degree to which their efforts had benefited shareholders. It became a benchmarking tool with which to project stock values that might be achievable under a business plan with certain assumptions. Pursuing a particular investment opportunity might temporarily lower the price, for example, but management could show how much value the investment would add over the long term. Thus inactive shareholders had a more reasonable basis for making an informed decision on whether to hold on to their stock or sell some of it.

The formula also focused their attention on the factors that determine value in the business. For example, one of the components of the formula took into account real estate values, which shareholders thought fluctuated less than the earnings component. By following the trend in the formula price, shareholders learned that real estate values were not always constant, particularly in a recessionary economy or when interest rates are rising. The inclusion of supply-and-demand considerations, as well as tax costs, lessened the shareholders' desires to liquidate their portfolio.

Balancing capital needs and shareholder liquidity. Much has been written about why founders and second-generation owners do not do a good job of managing shareholder relations. The entrepreneurial management style is often secretive and does not evolve naturally in the third or fourth "coalition" generations into the more open style of communication that is necessary to deal with growing numbers of inactive shareholders.

During these later stages, the psychic and other intangible benefits of ownership that normally bind shareholders to the family company in earlier stages tend to weaken. Managers do not benefit as much from "the family effect"—the strong loyalty to and identification with the business that is characteristic of founding families. As a result, shareholders will evaluate their stock according to the same criteria they apply to other investments. When tensions arise, business owners have tended to consider only two conventional solutions to liquidity issues: sell the company or go public. Both of the traditional options have well-known disadvantages.

If implemented and communicated properly, ongoing liquidity programs reconcile the capital needs of the business with the liquidity needs of the shareholders throughout the evolution of a family business, so a crisis level is never reached. These programs preserve the pride of family ownership and still allow inactive shareholders to diversify investments and get needed cash.

An established share price that is regularly updated also facilitates estate planning. It enables shareholders to plan for potential estate tax burdens. When the formula share price is high, for example, shareholders may be interested in cashing in some stock or gifting shares to charities. If the price drops, they might transfer shares to family members.

The proliferation of shareholders with different needs and loyalties will likely result in growing pressure on managements to provide liquidity. Responsible family managers will react proactively with creative solutions. If family ownership is to be preserved for future generations, they must have the vision to see the liquidity trends in later-generation businesses and respond to them before the problems become acute and the options limited.

— *François M. de Visscher*

Conflict Resolution

Uncovering the hidden fears that cause arguments

To end the vicious cycle of pain that marks family fights, you must uncover the underlying issues. Here's how to recognize them.

TRADITIONAL METHODS of conflict resolution assume that people are truly fighting about what they say they are fighting about and that they want to resolve their problems rationally. Family arguments, however, are far more subtle and far less rational. Family members frequently conspire to sustain conflict because it helps them avoid something they fear might be even worse than the devil they know.

Conflicts that mask hidden fears tend to follow a predictable circular pattern (see the illustration "Cycle of conflict," right). By understanding it, you will be able to see the source of disputes for what they really are. As anxiety builds, family members initiate arguments that distract them from critical issues. The encounters escalate into destructive battles, which create more anxiety. Eventually tempers cool down. Sooner or later the family's unresolved dilemmas resurface and the cycle begins once again.

The only way to break this vicious pattern is for families to confront the very issues they have diligently avoided. Sometimes they know painfully well what those issues are and merely need a sensitive advisor to help them talk candidly and constructively. Other times families bury their most important problems so deeply that they need a family therapist.

In the case of one family, the Spyros (a fictitious name), a terminally ill father and two sons had fallen into a regular pattern of squabbling. A consultant asked the family a series of "what if" questions, concluding with: "What would it feel like if Ted [the father] weren't yelling?"

The answer was startling. When the gravely ill patriarch yelled at his sons, the family could pretend he was well again.

Unaddressed fears can often be identified by asking, "What would happen if...?" For example, the Spyro sons could be asked, "What might happen if you weren't fighting about parking places?"

"We'd be fighting about something else."

"And what if you didn't fight about anything?"

"Then Dad wouldn't have any reason to yell at us."

Analyzing a chronic circular conflict can accomplish several things at once. After family members have identified their shared fears, they can begin to isolate the triggers that divert them into unproductive battles.

Although conflict can hurt a family and ruin a closely held business, it can also create opportunity. The greatest benefit of analyzing the cycle of repeated clashes is that family members learn routinely to ask one another, "What would happen if...?"

— *Kenneth Kaye*

Cycle of conflict

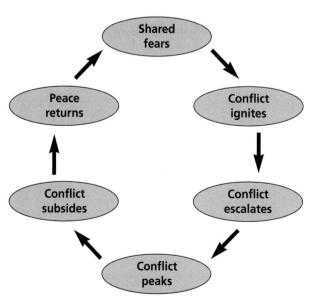

Mediation instead of court

Family business disputes involve a complicated mix of legal and emotional issues that should be kept out of court. There are several alternative ways to reach consensus, chief among them, mediation.

ALL HEALTHY ORGANIZATIONS have to deal with conflict, and a family business is no exception. In the typical first-generation company, the founder resolves disputes by fiat and acts as judge, jury, and enforcer. As the business expands and moves into the second generation, relationships among family members become more complex and new mechanisms are needed to handle the inevitable disagreements. Too often when the founder is no longer around, family conflict ends up in court.

Disagreements among family members in business usually involve a complex combination of legal and emotional issues which are best settled in private by the parties themselves. The matters in contention are often personal grievances dressed up as legal issues. Such problems cannot be constructively resolved by judicial trials.

There are alternative ways of resolving disputes. These processes can be lifesavers for family businesses threatened with divisive lawsuits. Unfortunately, many families do not know how such processes work, nor are they aware of the principal advantages and disadvantages.

The disadvantages of litigation are well known: Lawsuits are emotionally exhausting and usually result in win-lose outcomes based solely on narrow legal issues. They are also expensive.

The most common and least disruptive way of resolving conflicts is by negotiation between the family members, before the case goes to court. Yet, the ability to settle deep, emotional issues through negotiation requires a maturity and wisdom that is sometimes lacking.

Once they see their legal bills start to mount, however, family members may become more conciliatory. At some point in the pre-trial maneuvering, one litigant may try to open the door to negotiation by making a settlement offer through his attorney. But because such an offer is typically conducted through a series of telephone calls and letters, the process is often slow and ineffective. A major hindrance to a settlement may also be the lawyers themselves, whose training is geared to advocacy on behalf of a client and not the art of compromise.

The best alternative is mediation. This is an informal, voluntary process in which both sides agree to use a neutral third party to assist them in reaching an agreement. While the use of a neutral third party is not new, judges in many areas of the country have increasingly brought pressure on litigants to try it before resorting to a trial.

Mediation can take place either before court action is contemplated or after a court action has started. In both instances mediation allows the parties themselves to decide the outcome of the disagreement. The mediator has no vested interest in the outcome and is not bound by inflexible legal rules. He or she does not act as a judge but merely helps the parties search for settlement terms that are acceptable to both sides.

A mediator is thus free to search out hidden problems, to consider emotional issues, and to develop solutions based on the parties' true interests. Often just bringing the parties together at one time, in the same room, is all it takes.

If the parties are unwilling or unable to negotiate, they can consider arbitration. Arbitration is a more formal process in which both sides agree in writing to submit their dispute to a neutral third party. The arbitrator acts as judge and usually makes a binding decision that is final. In this process, the parties can structure the format to meet their needs. For example, they can choose to make the arbitrator's decision non-binding. The proceedings are private, both sides are usually represented by counsel, and a record is kept of the hearing.

The main disadvantage to the use of arbitration is that it gives a third party, who is not as familiar with the business and family dynamics as the parties themselves, the responsibility for making the final decision. In addition, many arbitrators tend to compromise and "split the baby down the middle."

How mediation works. The most desirable use of mediation is when the parties decide to do it on their own initiative, prior to beginning any legal action. The earlier a disagreement can be settled the better it is for the business and the family.

Once a mediator has been selected, he or she contacts both sides to establish a convenient time and place to conduct the session. To be successful, those who have decision-making or settlement authority must be present. It does little good to convince the president of a family company that the firm should pay a dividend to minority shareholders if Dad, the chairman, is the one who makes that decision and he is unwilling to participate in the sessions.

For the first meeting, the mediator brings all the

parties together in one room, explains the process, and establishes the ground rules. Next, the mediator asks participants on each side to fully explain their view of the disagreement and the issues involved. This is an important step, since it will probably be the first time that both sides have considered the other's point of view.

Emotions tend to run high during the initial part of the mediation process. The venting of feelings and frustrations at the opening session is encouraged by the mediator, who is attempting to determine the real issues involved. The opportunity to fully express one's view often produces a cathartic effect on the participants, which clears the air and allows the settlement process to move forward.

After all parties have stated their views, the mediator will usually separate the groups and meet with each side alone. During these sessions the mediator encourages candor and promises to keep confidential any private information disclosed to him. He urges the family members to identify and explain their real priorities, apart from the legal issues in the case. Does sister Claudia really want to force brother Fred out as chairman of the board? Or is she really more interested in receiving a pay raise and promotion for herself?

During the separate meetings, the mediator may challenge family members' perceptions of one another, which often trace back to childhood and are no longer valid. The mediator also acts as an agent of reality, correcting possible misinterpretations of statements made by the other side. As the discussions progress, he encourages the parties to honestly evaluate their underlying interests and to make reasonable settlement offers. Shuttling between rooms where the disputants wait, he communicates each offer and encourages counter-offers.

If the conflict can be resolved, an agreement will be drawn up that all parties sign. The agreement can then be enforced in court as a valid contract; it can be appealed only in exceptional circumstances, if, for example, it was based on fraud or material factual errors made in the mediation sessions.

If a settlement cannot be reached, the mediator will declare an impasse and the dispute will proceed to trial. The mediation sessions have not been recorded, and, at trial, neither side may introduce details of the various settlement offers as evidence against the other side.

Advantages to mediation. By participating in the decision-making, the parties feel responsible for the final outcome. They are also more likely to grasp the realities of their situation and are more open to accepting a reasonable settlement offer.

The mediation process does not dwell on the past and try to assign blame for what has happened. It looks to the future and seeks solutions from the parties themselves which will help restore damaged family relationships.

Some other advantages of mediation:

Guaranteed privacy. This provision is of particular importance to the typical family business, which likes to keep financial information and the personal lives of family members out of the media.

Retained control. In a family company, it seldom makes good business sense to give an outsider, such as a judge or arbitrator, control over important decisions that could affect the company. The best decisions can be made by family members themselves.

Quick decisions. Most mediations can be scheduled to begin within a month and can be completed in one to three sessions. When a settlement is reached, the agreement is enforceable as a contract. This permits family members to put the disagreement behind them and get on with business and their lives. When the parties resort to litigation, they can be tied up in court for years.

Relatively low costs. The costs of mediation depend on the complexity of the case and the number of sessions. Depending on their background and qualifications, mediators usually charge an hourly rate of $100 to $175 or a daily rate of $800 to $1,200. The per-session expense is about the same as that for the deposition of a party in pretrial discovery, which includes the lawyer's fee and a transcription of the testimony.

There are some instances when mediation is not appropriate. For example, a mediator must postpone or discontinue mediation when it becomes evident that a full disclosure of material facts has not been made by one of the parties. Likewise, if a power imbalance between the parties exists—and the weaker side is not represented by counsel—the mediator may decide not to proceed. Some parties are not capable of negotiating for themselves because of emotional problems, lack of training, timidity, or chemical dependency. For example, mediation may be impossible when a minority stockholder who is young, immature, and financially unsophisticated is pitted against an experienced, aggressive CEO who has unlimited access to corporate resources.

Divorces also commonly present power imbalance

A mediator can uncover hidden problems and help the parties find an acceptable settlement.

problems. And as more states adopt community property laws, which require the division of assets when a marriage is dissolved, divorces are increasingly becoming a major threat to the stability of a family business.

Choosing a mediator. The growing cadre of professional mediators includes numerous lawyers and retired judges. But many of the best and most experienced mediators do not come from legal backgrounds. The Society of Professionals for Dispute Resolution in Washington, D.C., has studied the problem of mediator qualifications and has determined that there are no specific degree requirements for a good mediator. At present there are no bar exams or national accreditation programs for mediators.

To be effective, a mediator must be a neutral outsider who is perceived as impartial by all parties. The family lawyer, accountant, or banker is usually not the ideal choice. These professionals are rarely trained in mediation, and their past association with the business and various family members tends to compromise the perception of their neutrality. However, these service providers are often familiar with the mediation process and can frequently recommend good mediators. Many modern attorneys and law firms now recognize dispute resolution processes as useful alternatives to litigation and are able to advise clients on when and how to use the appropriate procedures.

For family business disputes, the mediator should be knowledgeable about business, sensitive to the unique problems faced by family groups, and experienced working with owner-managers. A good mediator will be attuned to the emotional issues in family disputes and have the skill to design creative solutions to resolve family business problems. If a gender issue is involved, using male and female co-mediators can be helpful.

The personal styles and expertise of mediators vary, so you have to shop around to find one who is right for you.

The American Arbitration Association, which has offices around the country, is one of the best sources of names of qualified arbitrators and mediators. The association also publishes various helpful background materials, such as "A Guide to Mediation for Business People." Another national organization, the Center for Public Resources in New York City, also maintains lists of mediators. Finally, some of the best mediators can be found at regional firms, such as Judicate, based in Philadelphia; the Bates Edwards Group, with offices in San Francisco, San Diego, and Portland, Oregon; and Endispute, in Cambridge, Massachusetts, New York City, and Washington, D.C.

— *John S. Powell*

Nonfamily help in a family conflict

Most nonfamily managers stay out of family squabbles. But they can play useful roles in resolving conflict. Here's advice to them...which owners can use, too.

MOST FAMILY CONFLICTS ARE RESOLVED before anyone outside of the immediate family is aware of them. However, some family businesses are laden with friction and every now and then, even in the best-run businesses, a squabble may escalate and drag in nonfamily employees.

The question is, what should you, as a respected nonfamily executive in the family business, do then? Your first instinct may be to lay low and let the dispute run its natural course. Although this might feel prudent (and safe), you are likely to be sucked into the situation in some fashion or, at least, be affected by it.

Rather than being forced to assume a reactive posture, you would be smart to take control over your entry into the fray. You can dictate when you get involved. But choose carefully—your timing and approach can make a tremendous difference in how your contribution is received and in whether or not the conflict is resolved constructively.

Usually, the sooner you can become the referee, the better. A conflict in its embryonic stage is much easier to resolve. Of course, it's always best if your assistance is solicited by all parties involved in the dispute. As the old counseling maxim goes: "Help not perceived as help is not help."

A note of caution: Such fights frequently bear not only on the substantive issues of the conflict, but also on the relationships involved (for example, between parents and children or between siblings). Family members in a dispute may be struggling with issues of trust, control, autonomy, separation, emotional openness, and self-esteem. This overlap of family emotions and business disagreements make family fights more complicated than those that normally take place in the business setting. Recognizing this, you shouldn't intervene in situations that are too emotionally laden or are primarily the result of heavily conflicted family situations. Professional help is required under these circumstances.

If you've decided that it's appropriate and worthwhile to intervene, there are a number of roles that you can assume to help unfreeze the family's problem situation. These roles fall into two categories: task roles and maintenance roles.

Task roles enable you to work directly on the problem confronting the family group:

Information giver—providing new facts or additional data about issues.

Information seeker—asking questions to secure more data and a better understanding of different facets of the situation.

Clarifier—explaining facts in a way that makes them clearer.

Summarizer—pulling together ideas, facts, and suggestions in an effort to reach agreement.

Decision tester—seeking consensus on a decision.

Maintenance roles help you encourage the family members by making them feel good about working together on their problems:

Initiator—stimulating the group to take new directions or a different perspective on the problem situation.

Encourager—commending the family members' progress and helping them to believe that the problem is resolvable.

Harmonizer—mediating differences among the family members.

Some simple guidelines will help you succeed in each function: Avoid taking sides; get the participants in the dispute to focus on and stick to the issues; provide range of alternatives, instead of single answer; don't make the decision, facilitate decision making; and secure agreement from all participants on the decision or resolution to the problem before concluding any meeting.

In their seminal book on negotiations, *Getting to Yes*, Roger Fisher and William Ury recommend a four-step methodology for effective problem-solving. These steps are: separate the people from the problem; focus on interests, not position; invent options for mutual gain; and insist on using objective criteria to reach conclusions.

If you're going to function well as a mediator, this book is well worth reading. It's short, understandable, and full of solid advice that you will find useful to help others achieve agreement without giving in.

If you have the organizational status and the right skills, you have a responsibility as a respected outsider to help resolve family business disputes. It's in your own best interests as well as those of the business. The firm that you save may be the family's. The job that you save may be your own.

— *Edwin T. Crego Jr.*

Sibling Teams

How to succeed as co-managers

Co-management is tough to pull off, but it can work if siblings agree on roles, segment areas of responsibility, and agree on rules for resolving disagreements.

AS MORE BUSINESSES are passed to a second generation, a crucial question arises: Can siblings who are all ambitious and committed to the business really share power, or will lingering feelings of competition, rivalry, and jealousy inevitably pull them apart?

The potential for friction is aggravated in a second generation, when brothers and sisters are in line to take over a business. This has its roots in the siblings' life-long need for parental approval, which begins in childhood. Early battles over who gets the best toy or the largest piece of cake can surface later on in the business as resentment over allocation of stock, perks, and titles. The traditional model for success is "winner take all"; the parent names one of his offspring, most often the eldest son, to head the firm, and the others accept subordinate roles. Then, as the founder gradually withdraws from the business, the siblings are left to define their roles and responsibilities.

Shared sibling management is possible, but only with better planning by both the founder and his offspring than most firms normally do.

Co-management is not without its detractors, who maintain that there must be a single leader, and that shared authority is at least inefficient if not unworkable. But it is nonetheless a growing trend, in family businesses as well as the rest of corporate America. For example, at Fel-Pro Inc., a $230 million company in Skokie, Illinois, three members of the fourth generation, Kenneth Lehman, Dennis Kessler, and David Weinberg, share the title of president. The company, a manufacturer of gaskets and sealing products founded in 1918, has become ever more profitable in recent years and has received a number of awards for quality manufacturing(and, notably for excellence in management.

Like the three presidents of Fel-Pro, Jerry Scolari and his brother, Joey, have equal control over Scolari's Warehouse Markets, a chain of 16 grocery stores based in Sparks, Nevada. The Scolari brothers rotate the title of president every May, when their fiscal year begins. Joey is, in fact, chief executive officer and Jerry, chief operating officer. The shared presidency has mainly symbolic importance, emphasizing to employees and store managers, says Jerry, that the brothers "make all our business decisions together."

One of the reasons shared management has worked at both Fel-Pro and Scolari's is that the people now at the helm took over gradually from the previous generation. Succession should not be a sudden, wrenching event, as it is in too many businesses. Under the best of circumstances, it is planned and carried out in stages, over a period of 5 to 10 years. In this time, the older generation can play a crucial role in helping their successors define their separate responsibilities and set up ground rules for teamwork.

The process of working out roles has another benefit: During this time, it should become apparent which siblings are deeply committed to both the success of the business and the welfare of the family, and which are not. Only the most committed siblings should eventually be put in charge, whether the family opts for one or more chief executives.

Long-term success, however, depends on whether siblings can remain equal bosses and still retain individual control over their segments of the business. For many siblings, creating such "peerness" and "separation" is the most difficult issue they must resolve.

Peerness is a term to describe the level playing field that can be created for adult siblings working in the same business. It implies that all are equals in terms of influence and contribution to the company, even though each has a separate turf which he or she can dominate. It is often very hard for siblings to achieve separation in business because families, in their desire for closeness, often pressure siblings to erase differences and focus on sameness. Achieving both peerness and separation is difficult because it calls on people to live with ambiguity. They need to be able to act decisively, to take initiative, yet remain team players.

For owners who decide to pass the family business to more than one sibling, the question remains: how? One common approach is to split the company into divisions and give each sister or brother the responsibility of running one of them. Another is to create subsidiaries or new product lines for different children to manage. The family can develop a multiple presidency, in which siblings function as a top management team, or it can rotate the presidency, as the Scolari brothers do. Finally, when the company has a trusted senior executive who isn't a family member, he can be named president and the children can be given equal status with the title of vice-president.

The big problem in many family companies is that the members' separate responsibilities are never rigorously spelled out. More importantly, even when they are, old conflicts between siblings can often undermine peerness and teamwork.

The efforts of two brothers to achieve a working relationship on equal terms in a $25 million graphics business illustrates what can be done. The founder of the business—let's call him Carl Davis—was 62 and wanted to slow down a bit. Although he was ready to loosen his ties to the day-to-day operations of the firm, conflict between his two sons, Carl Jr. and Bud, prevented him from doing so.

Carl Jr., 38 had always been "just like his father." He was highly visible within the company and aggressive about having things done his way. As a boy he would go with his father to the office on weekends, and as a teenager had an after-school job in the warehouse. He had always known that his father expected him to be part of the business and he loved it.

Bud, 36, was an accommodator, more willing to adjust his views after hearing what others had to say, which was what he had always had to do with a brother like Carl. As a boy, whenever Bud tried to assert himself, Carl would argue him down. Years later, it wasn't too different. Carl would have a very clear idea of how things ought to be in the business. But Bud would often have to moderate Carl's extreme viewpoint and then sell it to others in the company.

The father and Carl Jr. had always been very close, and Bud had always felt like an outsider. The conflict between the two brothers had been bubbling up for years. Arguments became increasing common, ranging from sales strategies to where to put the Christmas tree. If Carl Sr.

was going to pass the business to his sons, he had to resolve their long-standing differences and old resentment. Both Carl Jr. and Bud felt strongly that the business should stay in the family, and knew it was up to them to work out their problems so that it would.

After several conversations it became clear that if Carl Jr. and Bud were going to co-manage the company, they would have to modify old rules and behaviors. They would also have to clearly delineate areas in which they would make joint decisions, and other areas where they could make independent ones. The very dialogue that was necessary to define their positions, moreover, forced the brothers to communicate and made them more aware of the issues that had divided them in the past. It also encouraged them to experiment with new roles that might lead to more productive relations. Whenever the brothers could not resolve an issue, the father, Carl Sr., acted as a "tiebreaker" in these planning sessions.

The Davis brothers agreed to make all strategic decisions jointly. They decided to "fire" Carl Sr. from his role as tiebreaker, and adopt a system of circuit breakers to prevent disagreements from escalating. Before a discussion got too hot, they would stop and let the issue sit for two to five days, during which time they would seek counsel from others. They would repeat this, if necessary, three times. If they still could not agree, they would call in a consultant. And if they could not work it out with a consultant, they would consider the decision a "no go"— they would make no decision.

> *Co-managers should control separate areas, but make tradeoffs for the common good.*

The brothers were confident that their long-term planning would carry them over the short-term bumps. They also recognized they held extremely different points of view on the use of new technologies in the plant. To develop a plan for the business, they hired a technology consultant. Once again, they had purposely inserted a buffer to reconcile their differences.

The brothers agreed that their salaries and perks would be equal. In addition, a committee of the board of directors was appointed to review the performance of the brothers, and a family council was established to improve communications with spouses and other relatives.

Being equal bosses isn't for everyone. The key to being able to function in this way is commitment. The co-managers must continually exchange information and trade off individual wants for the common good. It takes a lot of work, but it can be energizing and dynamic.

— *Barbara Hollander*

Improving Communication

Breaking barriers to give-and-take

The biggest obstacles to better communication are hidden agendas, procrastination, and fear of expressing emotions. Recognizing these, and eliminating them, must occur before communications can improve.

PEOPLE WHO INVEST IN REAL ESTATE say the key is "location, location, location." The key to success in maintaining a family business is "communication, communication, communication." Yet many families never get to first base in addressing communications issues, even those that realize how important it is to the outcome of the game.

One of the biggest obstacles to communication in families is hidden agendas. A father's hidden agenda may be that he has no intention of ever letting go. But a son's failure to confront his father on the succession issue may result from a hidden agenda, too; it may be that he really doesn't care for the responsibilities of leadership, and doesn't have the courage to say so.

A second block to communication results from waiting too long to address the issues. With the passage of time, small silences can grow into a mountain of guilt and rationalization. On the one hand, the father may be thinking, "I should have dealt with this years ago, and I have let it go too long. Now I am too embarrassed to deal with it." On the other hand, the son may be thinking that, absent any word to the contrary from Dad, his entitlement to the top job grows with every passing day.

A third and critical block is the feeling that the issues are so highly emotional that they seem to preclude any rational discussion. When a son has invested 20 years of his life in the hope of eventually running a business, any talk of succession with his father is bound to be power-

fully charged for both.

Real communication has an element of vulnerability to it. So if the son goes to Dad and tells him about his concerns for the future, he may hear something he doesn't want to hear. Yet it is far more risky to the relationship—and to the son's future—to let issues fester.

Questions about the competence of children pose some of the greatest challenges to family communication. For a while, parents can rationalize away doubts about competence as "a maturity problem," "an attitude problem," or "the influence of his friends." By the time children reach 30, however, parents should know whether their offspring have what it takes or not. If the parents don't know, the children have to be tested; they should be given more responsibility, and the chance to fail. Parents need to stop rescuing children. The children have to be subject to serious evaluation by outsiders—managers and personnel experts who can give them objective feedback. The next 10 years are critical in a young adult's life. Without good communication in the family, members of the next generation may hang on to illusions about their future in the business.

The father and son in my example have a lot of work to do. Ten years ago Dad probably could have eased his son out of the business without causing an uproar in the family. That would have made it possible to prepare a professional manager to run the company when father was ready to retire. Now it is too late. The son has few career alternatives. Because Dad has not dealt with the issue for so long, he has lost a lot of his moral authority. He knows it and feels powerless.

The father has to separate issues of authority in the business from the son's need to save face. He has to find a way of giving authority to those who are most able to provide competent leadership, while leaving his son with an adequate measure of self-esteem. Perhaps the son could be put in charge of a smaller entity such as one plant, for example. Or he could have a seat on the board and continue to draw a good salary, while professional non-family managers run the company.

Both father and son have to look for win-win alternatives that can extricate them from the dilemma that has led to mutual avoidance of the issues.

The situation demands an enormous amount of communication, patient problem solving, and compassion. Sadly, such qualities are frequently beyond the emotional resources of some families. The leader then faces the awful choice of saving the business or the relationship.

— *Peter Davis*

Watch your language and it will improve

Next time you address employees or family, listen to what you're saying. Avoid common pitfalls in the way you criticize or talk to the kids and develop the following habits.

THE WAY TO CORRECT a harmful communication pattern is to first recognize it as such, then explicitly change it. Some techniques:

Talk in the "first person." Use "I" and "we" more than "you" when approaching sensitive subjects. Overuse of "you" tends to be taken as accusatory and confrontational, as in "You should know better," or "You weren't listening." In contrast, framing a problem in terms of your own reaction is less offensive: "Did I forget to mention how important it was that these orders go out?" or "I feel hurt when my ideas are disregarded."

Pinpoint specifics. People are less defensive when reminded of a single instance of neglectful behavior than when they are told they are incompetent. Most of us will admit to one mistake, but resent generalized assertions about our character or ability. You can use specific instances to make a larger point about overall behavior, however.

Acknowledge that you may have been part of the problem. You can be generous and suggest, for example, that "Maybe my instructions weren't clear." Or, if appropriate, you can indicate you should have brought an issue up sooner: "I know I should have said something earlier, so it's partly my fault."

Collaborate on a solution. Think of creative ways to solve a problem together. Remember, it's the problem—not the people—who are on the examination table.

When criticized, paraphrase what a person is telling you. Show you understand the reasons why someone is criticizing you, and how he or she feels about the issue being raised. For example: "So you're angry with me because you think I humor you and don't really listen?"

In response to general criticism, ask for specifics. "Were you angry mostly because I forgot to send those invoices out after you told me they were important?"

Agree with facts. "You're right. I did forget to mail the invoices after you emphasized their importance."

Make a sincere effort to understand a critic's perception, and admit when you're wrong. "Given these facts, I can see how you would think I'm not listening, when I say I'll do something and don't." This takes guts, but remember, admitting to a single mistake does not imply lack of competence or character. In the long run, such an admission shows strength of character and earns respect.

How to criticize

There are no new tricks on giving constructive criticism. The good news is that the old guidelines still work, whether you're criticizing your own children or your partners'. So listen up:

Be sure that criticism is necessary. Sometimes people who know each other as well as you all do feel they should point out every little mistake, even when they know that will just cause an emotional reaction. Criticize only repeated patterns of behavior, not single aberrations.

Phrase your criticism to help, not hurt. Criticism should improve your relationship with the kids. Point out the specific behavior—privately—as soon as possible after it occurs. If you carry around a list of criticisms going way back to a forgotten birthday, you'll only cause resentment.

Do not tell the kids that they "always" or "never" do something. This may be taken as an indictment of their personality rather than criticism of specific behavior. No amount of compliments will make up for the damage that is caused by criticizing a loved one's personality.

Put your criticism in as positive a context as you can. For example, let's say a daughter is too stubborn to change the way she's been scheduling production. Instead of telling her that she's stubborn, why not give her a strong personal incentive to change, like: "If you gave the new schedule a fair chance, you might find it works much better than you think. And if that's so, your job will be much easier. You'll have time to get more involved with management decisions…"

Under ideal circumstances, the giver and receiver of criticism both learn something from the exchange and are drawn closer together by it.

How to talk to "the kids"

Parents must watch their tongues when talking to the younger generation if they want their sons and daughters to mature in the business. Below, some tips on language to avoid:

Don't call sons and daughters "kids," and don't address them by nicknames. If you do, the son or daughter, and other employees, will read it to mean: "The kids are still kids, even though they may be managers, vice-presidents, or directors."

Don't tell a son or daughter, "You're not ready for that," or, "This is the way we've always done it." It will be read: "Remember who's in control here."

Never remind offspring: "I'm the one who's paying your salary," or, "I'm giving you this bonus." Such language indicates that a son or daughter's compensation is based on the parent's benevolence, not on his or her performance. A clear recital of the recipient's achievements, of the reasons the increase is deserved, will do more to boost self-esteem.

Avoid all variations of the cliché: "Someday, son, all this will be yours." Read: "There is no real succession plan at this company."

Also avoid another harmful cliché: "I've built this business from the ground up, and you want to change it after you're one year out of business school." Read: "Education is not as valuable as experience."

— *Andrea Grace Mackiewicz*

Techniques for constructive conversation

1. The sun should never set on an emotionally significant issue that remains unresolved. Avoid letting issues fester until they get too hot to handle.

2. Find the right time and place to talk seriously. Avoid the interruptions at work.

3. Before opening your mouth, clarify in your mind what you want and what is fair to other family members. Be sure about the principles you want to adhere to.

4. Seek objective advice on your own possible hidden agendas, and on the best way to frame the issues. Once the issues are on the table, look for alternative win-win solutions that address both business and family needs and promise a way out of the dilemma.

5. Family members should agree on what will be expected of successors-to-be, and on measures to determine whether those expectations are being met. Potential successors should be given frequent feedback.

6 .Before assigning blame for something, ask yourself what you contribute to the problem. Remember that the person you have the most power to change is yourself.

7. Keep the discussions moving forward. Be willing to negotiate. Remember that other family members may not be ready to hear you. It may take years for them to unfreeze. Stick with it. Build goodwill through your openness.

— *Peter Davis*

Family Councils

Creating unity with a family council

Even the most extended family can satisfy diverging needs by starting a family council, writing a family creed, and keeping people focused on crucial issues. Here's how.

IT HAPPENS ALL TOO OFTEN: Entrepreneurs start new businesses and succeed their wildest dreams. But rather than adding to the quality of family life, the business threatens to destroy it. Some firms, however, succeed in bringing the family closer together.

Family strategic planning can help families approach their business in a unified way, rather than as a group of individuals who happen to be related. It can be valuable in building the business and helping family members cope with inevitable stresses.

Family strategic planning is not the same thing as business planning, which usually is done in other forums that may include nonfamily managers; rather, it is concerned with improving communication in the family and laying a strong foundation for resolving differences and keeping the peace. Through planning, the family establishes policies that govern the relationship of their home and business lives and spell out the responsibilities of the members to one another and the business.

The first step is to establish a council that permits family members to express their aspirations, views, and concerns (perhaps for the first time) and allows them to participate in policy-making. The council is simply a forum. Setting one up does not mean that the business becomes a democracy and the owner gives up the last word. Family councils usually act responsibly, and it is rarely necessary for owners to exercise their veto powers.

At least in spirit, however, a council establishes that the company is a family business rather than "dad's business." The family members are likely to gain a better understanding of the owner's perspective and to learn to appreciate that the business doesn't just provide rewards, but also demands responsibility.

The strong bond of affection in most families usually permits them to resolve their differences themselves. For these families, regular meetings in a council give them the opportunity to talk openly and set up rules. The chances of misunderstandings are greatly reduced, and the rules are most likely to be respected when they are arrived at through consensus rather than edict.

Every family has to decide for itself who should participate. Some prefer to include only family members who are active in the business; however, unless there are strong reasons to the contrary, the council will be most effective if both active and inactive family members *and their spouses* are invited to take part. All family members usually have some stake in the business, even if indirect; spouses are going to find out what is discussed anyway, so they might as well hear it first-hand and accurately. For them, a council meeting can be an eye-opening experience, because they probably never really understood what was going on.

Don't wait too long to get started. Family council meetings should begin as soon as the kids are old enough to enter the business. An ideal way to inaugurate a council is with a one-day family retreat at a quiet place away from the shop. You might also want to bring along an experienced family business consultant to conduct these initial

Who should be on the council?

The composition of a family council changes depending on the ownership form and stage of development of the company. For example:

In a first-generation, owner-managed company, the family council would typically be made up of the founder, his or her spouse, and their children.

In a second generation, sibling-partnership company, the council would be composed of the sibling partners and their spouses.

In a second generation or beyond, cousin-syndicate company, the council would be made up of representatives from the various branches and generations of the extended family. *— Ivan Lansberg* sessions. Although the family itself must make the decisions, a consultant is a seasoned and objective guide who can help lay out the questions that should be addressed, assure that the discussion is organized and not just a bull or gripe session, and set the tone for future meetings.

The owner should state at the outset that family members are free to express whatever is on their minds, that "anything goes." He should also make it clear that he is at the meeting as a participant, not as the parent/boss. In this atmosphere, family members can express pent-up emotions that could prevent agreement on a policy.

In our experience, this rarely results in unpleasant confrontations and usually has a cathartic effect. At one meeting, two daughters who were not active in the business brought an extra supply of tissues, expecting a teary session. Although they sat on the board of directors, they had never been offered the same opportunities in the business as their brother and resented his patronizing attitudes and "bullying" at board meetings. Once their feelings were allowed to surface, their concerns were addressed and the family was able to develop a creed that all could accept and abide by.

A family creed is the council's next project. This document spells out your family's values and basic policies in relation to the business, and becomes the basis of the family strategic plan. Before it can be written, the family must address a number of critical issues (see "The Family Council Agenda" below). Many families after a day-long retreat are able to develop a first draft, which is then "ratified" by the members at a later meeting. The creed should be a living document that is reviewed at least once a year and can be expanded or amended as new problems arise, new members come into the family, and new points of view appear. Having established it, the family can then monitor their progress, as measured against the values in the creed, at periodic meetings.

The retreat should be the beginning rather than the end of family communication. A timetable should be set for future meetings, which can be for two or three hours rather than full day. Some families have annual day-long meetings with guest speakers. Responsibilities for organization and leadership of the meetings can be rotated among family members, and you may want to invite the company lawyer, accountant, or insurance agent as guests to explain topics of interest. If you have an independent board of directors, a joint meeting with them can also be productive.

As your family council and creed have confirmed, your family business is unique. No other enterprise has the same character, beliefs, values, and skills; and certainly nobody else has the same family.

If you can reach agreement on the critical issues, your family will have established a strong foundation for future understanding. If not, you will have identified the issues and be able to work toward resolving them.

— *Benjamin Benson, Edwin T. Crego Jr.*
& Ronald Drucker

The family council agenda

A well designed family strategic plan usually deals with all or most of the following critical questions:

The family's mission: What are the family's aspirations for the business? Do we want to keep it in the family? Sell it eventually? Go public?

Management standards for the business: In the management of the business, which should be paramount—the best interests of the family, the best interests of the business, or some combination?

Involvement of family members in the business: What should be the criteria for entry? Should in-laws be allowed to enter? How should family members be compensated? How should they be evaluated? What if they don't perform up to appropriate standards? How will the roles of family members in the business be determined?

Ownership of stock in the business: Who will be allowed to own stock in the company? Who should have voting control? Who should share in the future appreciation of the stock? What should be our dividend policy? What will happen to stock ownership in the next generation? Should we differentiate between family members who are active in the business and those who are inactive?

Management succession: What should be the criteria for selecting the next leader? When will the transition take place? What should be done if the choice turns out to be wrong?

What are the owner's aspirations in retirement? How can we help him or her to achieve them? How can we insure the owner's financial security in retirement?

Relationships with one another: What responsibilities do we have toward one another? How can we best attain an atmosphere that enhances mutual respect and support? How should we deal with differences between family members?

Relations with others: Should we have an independent board of directors? If so, how should our family relate to it? How can we protect the security of loyal and valuable employees? What are our responsibilities to the community?

Nonfamily Managers

What to tell execs... before you hire them

When negotiating with potential managers, be sure to discuss with them what it means to work in a family company. It will open their eyes, helping both of you to gauge whether there's a good match.

THE COMPANY'S TEAM of professional managers plays an essential role in a profitable business, and in assuring a smooth transfer of leadership to the next generation. Yet, when business owners are hiring their team, the discussions usually focus myopically on short-term operational goals and not on the long-term structure and needs of both the family and the business. The result is too often a disaster waiting to happen.

No matter how capable or loyal, the nonfamily manager in a family business must usually accept that his upward mobility will be limited by family considerations. A hired gun will, in most cases, always be a hired gun. The professional manager can never set his sights on running the company when owners have competent heirs. Why, then, would any manager with brains and top credentials want to work in a family company at all?

For the right person, a well-managed, successful, and happy family business offers certain advantages and opportunities. The pay is usually competitive and a manager can have more real influence on major decision-making than in larger public companies. The feeling of making a truly important contribution is a reward.

In addition, most family firms are in it for the long haul, which is the loyal manager's best guarantee of long-term security and well-being.

In the best of possible worlds, the professional becomes a member of a family that appreciates loyalty and hard work, and shares the benefits of its success. Key managers in a family firm report directly to the owners. They are valued for their technical knowledge and skill, in marketing, finance, manufacturing—whatever. But personal chemistry is most important in a family firm. If a per-

son can't admire the family and its values, then he or she should have the integrity not to apply. It is imperative that nonfamily management share the business owner's dream and basic values.

Ideally, an owner will find someone in his mid- to late 40s or early 50s who has at least 20 years of experience with other companies and has 15 to 20 years or more to give to the company. Don't pinch pennies. While the psychic rewards of working in a family company can be great, experienced managers will not willingly sacrifice their standard of living for the challenges offered. Too often, if they accept a cut in pay, they usually regret it later on, become unhappy, and eventually become unproductive.

The idea that you don't have to pay competitively but can attract top people by giving them a "piece of the action" is a common delusion. What does it mean to own 10 percent of the stock in a company that pays no dividends (and for which there may be no market)? The manager eventually could hit the jackpot if the stock triples in value and the business is sold. But when the company is sold, he usually loses his job. Better to give him the incentive of salary increases, which he can invest himself.

Misperceptions about pay are only one cause of broken marriages. A more fundamental problem in the hiring process is that neither party is mindful enough of what the future holds.

Sometimes when the aging owner has children who are too young or insufficiently trained to take over, the key manager may have to take on the role of regent. Under this scenario, he must lead the company as the head of a caretaker regime while preparing the heirs for their responsibilities. Unfortunately, the subject is rarely mentioned in interviews with managerial applicants. The coming of the crown prince or princess thus becomes a sudden, anxiety-ridden event. The key manager is forced to take on the role of mentor to sons and daughters whose arrival threatens his own position. Or the regent is suddenly thrust in the middle of a battle for control between warring siblings that he is not equipped to handle.

For all these reasons, business owners should tell applicants all they can about family goals and politics before offering the job. The candidates should meet not only the children who are potential heirs to the business and will one day be their bosses, but also children who are not active in the business.

The presence of competent successors in the business is any professional's best security blanket. If there are no potential successors, the owners should talk frankly with applicants about the family's future plans for the business.

But key managers will also be looking for other possible guarantors of their future security and opportunity to contribute within the company. For example, the existence of an independent board of outside directors can assure them of a forum in which their performance will be appraised objectively.

The business owner who wants to hire top people should marshal evidence of his commitment to his managers, to professionalism, to "continuing this business forever." Do you have a succession plan? Does the company have a management development plan? A pension plan? Do you have an open accounting system? Do you pride yourself on open communication, on not hiding anything from key people? These are all points to emphasize in interviews with candidates.

Key managers are often the bridge between generations, providing the stability to get over the inevitable bumps in succession. As in many marriages, however, when the courtship is too short and the partners don't think enough about their future together, the relationship may end up on the rocks.

— *Léon Danco*

Sharing sensitive information

What your managers don't know can come back to haunt you. It is also frustrating and stressful for them.

YOU WON'T FIND THE COMMANDMENT, "Thou shalt maintain an orthodox accounting system and make available the data therefrom to thine officers and managers," anywhere in religious books. But it is high on the list of absolute requirements for success in a family business.

The costs of hiring a reputable accounting firm or installing management information systems may seem like a luxury to family owned firms. But nowadays you can't run a competitive, efficient business without information-sharing. As markets change, as old products die and new ones are born, as hungry new competitors emerge, information of all sorts must flow up and down the ladder faster, and the people responsible for making day-to-day decisions need to be trusted with sensitive data.

Yet there are still family companies that are reluctant to share vital information on the operation of the business with non-family senior managers. There are purchasing agents who don't know the total value of their inventory, managers of manufacturing who are not told what their indirect labor costs are or have not been shown the depreciation schedule for plant machinery. How can they run a business that way?

Such secrecy is, of course, needed if you have to cover up various tax ploys. Instead of making a profit, the goal of some companies seems to be to "break even higher and higher." As annual revenues and earnings increase, deductible expenses somehow seem to grow in order to keep pace with them.

In family businesses, the magic of bookkeeping covers up a lot of the "gravy," the bonuses and the perks that can supplement the owners' salaries but could appear questionable to the IRS. Mom writes the "confidential" checks which go to family officers but are not so identified in the general accounting system. But a reputable accounting firm and a professional CFO are usually too smart to go along with such games.

Though taxes are truly a burden, I believe the IRS code nonetheless can provide a useful moral standard. The code can also foster ethical practices and open systems of accounting that are essential to the survival of a family business. In the long run, it is cheaper and more efficient to share accurate information on a regular basis than to suffer the long delays of having it travel up and down the management hierarchy or to sow confusion by trying to run a business with an accounting system that is designed to confound the IRS and not provide reliable, objective perspective.

There are some kinds of information, of course, that might not be shared with middle management. If the board is considering closing a plant or a division, for example, it will only alarm employees unnecessarily to inform them in the early stages of the discussions before any decision is made. Likewise, you can't always share the company's long-term strategic plan or the design of a new product with everyone. In a competitive world, some documents are truly "confidential."

What many businesses that are not sophisticated at managing the flow of information do is to simply shut off the spigot entirely. The policy cascades back on the owner in the form of constant questions and requests for information. Every time managers need to know something, they must come to the boss. Which may be the way some owners want it—they like to believe in their own indispensability and to foster exactly this kind of dependence. But the frequent requests and questions also consume much time that an owner should be spending on more important things.

There has never been a company that was hurt by too much openness—and that includes sharing of "sensitive" financial data. There is one owner who informs his entire senior management group of where every dime in revenues goes. The company is an S corp and made $6 million in profits last year. It goes into the owner's pocket, along with an extra hundred thousand or two from bonuses and perks. The senior managers are fully aware that they're making him rich, but are they upset or resentful? Not in the least. Several of them earn as much as $250,000. They'll work their hides off this year, too, in hopes that the owner will make $7 million.

Most nonfamily managers tend to accept that they do not have a right to receive, and are never going to get, equity in a family company. They usually understand, too, that a son or daughter or other family member will get shots at the top positions in management before them. So long as those family members are qualified and capable and treat the managers with the respect they deserve, they accept the realities of working in a family firm. They accept, or they leave.

They do demand to be treated with decency and respect, however, and they do have a right to equal pay for equal work. The best companies will have open, fair salary schedules, based on industry standards, that ensure family and nonfamily employees are paid alike for the same work. Executive talent today is highly mobile. You can't get away with paying your son or daughter $100,000 a year and nonfamily managers $50,000 a year for doing the same supervisory job, not without losing some of your most capable people.

Just as important, senior managers have a right to know as well as a need to know. Surveys show that the psychological satisfactions from a job are just as important to managers as the money, sometimes maybe even more so. But not having enough information to do their job right is a source of frustration and stress.

Labor today still wants "more," as Samuel Gompers said, but they want more information as well as higher wages. If you can't trust senior managers with more knowledge, you should not give them less. You should

get rid of them.

Whether they know it or not, good businesses today are virtual universities. They must offer employees constant training and educational programs. The whole concept of empowerment is based on the conviction that an investment in a knowledgeable worker is an investment in productivity.

It's part of the cost of doing business, like paying rent.

— *Léon Danco*

Motivating your nonfamily managers

If you want to hang on to loyal nonfamily managers, it helps to understand how they rate your company as a place to work.

TODAY'S DISILLUSIONED EMPLOYEES in large corporations are changing careers and companies four or five times during their working years. Family businesses, once stereotyped as dead-ends for ambitious managers, are now looking better and better.

Of course, not all family businesses are ideal places for them to park their loyalty. The *Journal of General Management* reported that a survey of nonfamily executives in family businesses found their jobs to be a mixed bag. They identified strengths of their employers as: opportunity for quicker authority, responsibility, and participation in decision-making; personalized work environment; and peer group evaluation at the board of directors level. However, they also complained about weaknesses, such as lower starting salaries, lack of formal hiring practices, and nonfamily/family and interfamily managerial rivalry.

Does your family business offer security and the opportunity for career mobility and financial advancement? Here are six attributes nonfamily managers will use to rate your company:

Strong core values. Frequently, when the family's name is on the door, they have a stronger commitment than a faceless corporation to do what's right for customers and employees. One of the great things about a family business is that the core values of a family such as honesty, fairness, and responsibility for one's actions, can actually be reflected in the way business is done.

Clear mission. Successful family businesses clearly define their purpose: why they exist and what they want to accomplish.

Professional work environment. A mission statement is great, but it should go beyond lip service. A well run family business must have a strategic plan, effective management systems, and efficient operating plans and communications, all of which should reflect the company's mission.

Objective recognition and reward systems. The family business should also concentrate on maximizing employee contribution and commitment, by allowing nonfamily members to hold key management positions, assigning responsibilities and authority based on competence, and utilizing performance-based compensation. Specifically, the compensation package should include some combination of nondiscretionary performance- and profit-based compensation, incentive stock options, deferred compensation, and phantom stock, which is not really equity, but appreciates (or falls) with the price of the company's common shares.

Commitment to the customer. Excellent family businesses exemplify this trait. No matter how big they have grown, these businesses have remained externally focused and have kept bureaucracy to a minimum.

Innovative and entrepreneurial behavior. A key to long-term business survival is the ability to adapt and respond quickly. This requires continuous innovation and entrepreneurial type risks in responding to changes in the marketplace.

— *Edwin T. Crego Jr.*

– III –

COMPENSATION

IT'S A STRAIGHTFORWARD QUESTION: What should I pay myself, my family members, and my top nonfamily employees? The range of answers, however, is astounding, and the rationale for different schemes is more often subjective than not.

The only objective perspective comes from compensation data. This section—itself one large chapter—presents the results of several extensive family business compensation studies. Ranges and averages of pay and perks for family executives, top nonfamily managers, and board members are given. They are also compared with norms at public companies. The size of each employee's paycheck is up to each owner, but so many owners find themselves with little basis on which to make compensation decisions. These numbers should help.

The chapter also presents advice on two tough issues: What constitutes "fair" pay for family members, and how to reward key nonfamily employees without diluting family ownership of the company. Specific compensation techniques are explained.

What to pay yourself, family, and nonfamily

Salaries for top executives

Family businesses as a group should take note that their executives earn significantly less than their counterparts in nonfamily businesses.

EXECUTIVE COMPENSATION has been under intense scrutiny in the last few years. While news headlines question the validity of exorbitant salaries for certain high-profile CEOs, the debate within companies is whether their compensation packages are competitive enough to keep or attract the best talent, without going overboard.

As a result, many studies have been commissioned to provide data on executive compensation in public companies. But it is rare to find data on family businesses. To shed light on the situation, *Family Business* magazine and Coopers & Lybrand, the international public accounting firm, surveyed owners in 1994 on the levels of compensation and benefits for top executives and board members in their family businesses. Data was collected on more than 750 executives nationwide, in all types of industries, locations, and company sizes.

The results, summarized in the accompanying tables, are encouraging in some areas, but raise disturbing questions in others. The top executives in family businesses earn as much as their counterparts in nonfamily businesses, for example, but other top executives earn much less, and have very little opportunity for equity ownership. On the other hand, family companies pay the chairmen of their boards far more than nonfamily companies, and reward the rest of their board members very well.

Executive pay and benefits. The survey asked for salary and bonus figures for executives. The results for the top three executives, grouped according to the sizes of their companies, are shown on the next page in Tables 1, 2, and 3, respectively. Interestingly, the top executive at companies with less than $1 million in annual revenues earns exceedingly more than the top executives at companies from $1 to $20 million in size. Part of the reason may be that many of the smallest companies employ only a few people; the owners do all the work and have few constraints on what they pay themselves. Still, the average total compensation to these chief executives is $182,876, a sizable percentage of the firms' revenues.

Salaries for the second and third executive from the top follow a more conventional pattern; they are modest at smaller companies and rise steadily as company size increases. Bonuses build too, jumping significantly when companies surpass $20 or $50 million.

These figures should help family business owners gauge their compensation packages for top employees—and themselves—against other family firms. But family businesses as a group should take note that their executives earn significantly less than their counterparts in nonfamily businesses (Table 4), according to figures reported in published surveys. The average total compensation for the top family business executive, around $219,000, is comparable to that in nonfamily firms, but the compensation for all other executives lags greatly. The second through fifth highest executives in nonfamily businesses earn a base salary, on average, that is 27 percent higher than their counterparts in family owned businesses. Because bonuses for the two groups are similar, the gap narrows some when comparing total compensation, but nonfamily executives still make 17 percent more.

The good news is that benefits provided to executives in family companies closely track those in the general business community. The percentages of family businesses offering various benefits (Table 5) differs from

1. Compensation for top family executive

Company size (revenues)	Base salary		Average bonus	Average bonus as % of base	Total cash compensation	
	Mean	Median			Mean	Median
Less than $1M	$137,967	$144,000	$38,367	28%	$182,876	$150,000
$1M to $3M	79,349	75,000	7,812	10	86,391	90,300
$3M to $10M	103,001	100,000	34,943	34	138,389	146,000
$10M to $20M	115,662	96,000	81,438	70	197,330	126,691
$20M to $50M	142,833	130,000	167,807	117	300,403	159,000
Greater than $50M	241,250	236,000	169,504	70	413,004	336,000
All respondents	136,677	130,167	83,312	61	219,732	166,332

2. Compensation for #2 family executive

Company size (revenues)	Base salary		Average bonus	Average bonus as % of base	Total cash compensation	
	Mean	Median			Mean	Median
Less than $1M	$50,394	$40,000	$11,504	.23%	$65,608	$50,000
$1M to $3M	55,359	52,000	3,586	.6	58,945	55,000
$3M to $10M	74,599	78,000	22,629	.30	94,950	95,000
$10M to $20M	81,240	65,000	31,719	.39	113,113	84,350
$20M to $50M	94,492	86,000	24,113	.26	119,021	115,000
Greater than $50M	162,983	150,000	77,444	.48	240,427	180,000
All respondents	86,511	78,500	28,499	.33	115,344	96,558

3. Compensation for #3 family executive

Company size (revenues)	Base salary		Average bonus	Average bonus as % of base	Total cash compensation	
	Mean	Median			Mean	Median
Less than $1M	$46,640	$38,000	$4,229	9%	$56,769	$43,500
$1M to $3M	46,282	39,709	2,041	4	48,553	41,400
$3M to $10M	58,531	62,000	13,106	22	71,910	72,600
$10M to $20M	64,908	64,000	26,568	41	87,014	75,000
$20M to $50M	82,875	73,500	18,824	23	101,283	88,000
Greater than $50M	100,545	100,000	59,290	59	164,335	150,000
All respondents	66,630	62,868	20,676	31	88,311	78,417

4. Compensation: Family vs. nonfamily businesses

Position	Family owned			Nonfamily owned*		
	Average base salary	Average bonus	Average total cash compensation	Average base salary	Average bonus	Average total cash compensation
Top executive	$136,677	$83,312	$219,732	$169,735	$59,300	$219,540
Executive #2	86,511	28,499	115,344	122,070	30,760	150,030
Executive #3	66,630	20,676	88,311	94,270	19,950	125,000
Executive #4	60,490	16,750	78,010	85,245	17,030	99,780
Executive #5	56,260	10,960	75,135	75,725	13,575	86,550

Nonfamily data represents companies with revenues from $5 to $15 million, a central range against which to judge family businesses. Figures for family firms are from the Coopers & Lybrand survey. Figures for nonfamily firms are compiled from: Officer Compensation Report, A Panel Publication, 1994, New York; Finance, Accounting, and Legal Compensation Survey Results, 1991, William M. Mercer Inc., Deerfield, IL; Executive Compensation Middle Market Survey, 1991, Ernst & Young, New York; and Top Management Report, 1992, Wyatt Data Services, Fort Lee, NJ.

general business averages by less than 5 percent, from medical and life insurance all the way down the line to club memberships and use of a company car. Note that many benefits—for family and nonfamily companies—drop off steadily from the top position down. For example, only 50 to 60 percent of the companies surveyed offer even basics such as medical and life insurance and retirement plans to the fifth executive from the top. This curve is similar for all of business.

5. Benefits to top 5 executives
(Percent of all respondents providing the following)

	Executive				
Benefit	#1	#2	#3	#4	#5
Medical	94%	89%	82%	72%	64%
Dental	59	53	49	43	40
Eye care	23	20	18	16	14
Supplemental medical	21	18	12	9	9
Physical exams	26	19	16	10	10
Life insurance	82	70	65	56	50
Split dollar life	28	17	11	9	8
Supplemental life	19	15	11	10	6
Retirement plan	73	69	64	58	52
Supplemental retirement	15	9	8	6	3
Company car	58	49	38	25	24
Car allowance	22	22	24	19	15
Association memberships	44	34	23	19	19
Club memberships	23	15	9	6	3
Board fees	17	14	10	4	6
Other*	15	15	13	12	10

* Included financial planning services, pension plan options, and complimentary food.

Board member pay. Although family companies pay their top executives less than nonfamily companies do, they pay board chairmen significantly more. As shown in Table 6, fees to board chairmen averaged $35,863, and bonuses added $21,095 more, for a total of $61,567. This is far above the $26,740 average for total compensation in nonfamily companies. Typically in nonfamily businesses, directors don't receive bonuses; they usually receive a retainer plus a fee each time they attend a board or committee meeting.

Compensation declines sharply to $23,762 for the second ranking board member at family firms, which is comparable to the figure for nonfamily companies. The third position, which typically represents a general board member, receives about $13,000 a year.

Family business consultant Léon Danco says the reason board chairmen usually earn so much in family firms is that often "the chairman is not truly a director. He's usually an aging owner who is no longer managing the business. The kid is now president and the parent becomes chairman. This is just another way for the owner to take money out of the business."

Employee bonuses. Although family businesses pay executives less, they offer roughly equivalent bonuses, which makes them competitive on this score. But due to the prior lack of data, owners have had a difficult time deciding what factors to use to determine bonuses. Our survey reveals three factors that are critical, and all are used rather evenly. Table 7 indicates that management discretion, measurements of employee performance, and success in meeting preset objectives, are all important considerations in determining bonuses. The relative weight of these factors does not change much, either, in judging senior managers, middle managers, or general employees.

Equity and ownership. However, as Table 8 shows, amazingly few owners are willing to offer equity posi-

6. Board of directors compensation

Position	Is this a family member? (% yes)	Average ownership	Average annual fee received	Average last bonus	Average total cash compensation	Average total compensation in nonfamily businesses*
Chairman	93%	41%	$35,863	$21,095	$61,567	$26,740
Position #2	76	17	14,079	8,861	23,762	22,220
Position #3	68	12	9,159	2,145	13,259	N/A

* For companies with less than $25 million in revenue. Sources: Corporate Directors' Compensation, 1993 Edition, The Conference Board, New York; and Compensation for Outside Directors, 1991, Handy HRM Corp., New York.

tions to nonfamily employees. Family business really means family business. Even the highest ranking nonfamily employees are left out; only 4 percent of nonfamily executives receive stock grants, only 2 percent receive either stock options or phantom stock, and only 2 percent enter into partnerships. And in these cases, the average share of ownership reaches only 2 percent.

All other employees, from senior managers on down, are virtually written off from equity consideration.

As might be expected, family members dominate the top spot at family companies. Table 9 indicates their ownership share, too, is often significant, ranging from an average of 70 percent in companies doing less than $1 million to 31 percent at larger firms. In all size firms, family presence in the number two or three spot drops; in the smallest companies, family members fill 57 percent of the second-ranking positions and 30 percent of the third-ranking positions. The share of ownership for these people sinks to 10 and 7 percent, respectively.

Nevertheless, contrary to popular notions, the family presence in the top three positions remains significant as company size increases, even for firms earning more than $50 million a year. There is little drop-off in family involvement, or ownership percentage. Whether bigger is better or not, family control remains high.

Many family business owners want to compare their practices with other family firms. The data presented here should help a great deal. For owners who want to compare themselves with nonfamily companies, the scorecard looks like this: Family firms offer equivalent bonuses, equivalent benefits, and certainly compensate their board members favorably. Other than the chief, however, they are not paying top executives competitively, and are not providing equity opportunities to their key people.

— *Karen Sindelar*

7. Basis for employee bonuses
(Percent of all respondents that offer bonuses)

Employee type	Management discretion	Performance measures	Preset objectives	Other
Executive	50%	27%	20%	3%
Senior manager	29	33	33	5
Middle manager	29	31	31	9
Administrative employees	39	26	27	8
All employees	36	26	25	13

8. Equity of nonfamily employees
(Percent of all respondents providing the following)

Employee type	Stock grant	Stock option	Phantom stock	Partnership	Average % ownership
Executive	4%	2%	2%	2%	2%
Senior manager	3	0	0	0	1
Middle manager	1	0	0	1	0
Administrative employees	0	0	0	1	0

9. Family control and ownership

Company size (revenues)	Top executive Is this a family member? (% yes)	Average ownership	#2 executive Is this a family member? (% yes)	Average ownership	#3 executive Is this a family member? (% yes)	Average ownership
Less than $1M	83%	70%	57%	10%	30%	7%
$1M to $3M	100	31	62	16	46	4
$3M to $10M	100	50	86	15	77	12
$10M to $20M	92	41	54	9	69	12
$20M to $50M	88	35	54	12	46	9
Greater than $50M	92	43	50	12	27	1
All respondents	93	45	61	12	49	7

Fair pay for family members

Compensation should be based on performance, not sentiment. How to establish a rational system.

SOME FAMILY BUSINESS OWNERS purposely underpay children or relatives. They believe that the company's value—ultimately, to their kin and their children—grows as a consequence of their work. Also, they don't want anyone to think the boss is playing favorites with relatives.

Many family business owners, however, err on the side of overpayment, treating salaries, bonuses, and perks as matters of entitlement. Some owners pay their children on the basis of age, seniority, or the number of grandchildren their take-home checks support. Others pay equal salaries to all siblings, regardless of contribution. In very small businesses, family members who are paid at all are generally paid more than average. The owners are not just being generous; usually they feel guilty about laying a trip on offspring or relatives to

Misguided policies

These bad models are all too familiar:

Someday Enterprises "You're not making much now, but some day it'll all be yours." (No matter how little you contribute.)

Love, Duty & Co. Everyone is close, cooperative, and mutually supportive. But the future is left unspecified— and not to be discussed.

Fair Shares Holding Co. The compensation scheme, business roles, and expectations about future organization are designed for egalitarian treatment of siblings. They have little or nothing to do with business needs, individual abilities, and performance.

Marx Brothers From each according to his ability, to each according to his needs.

Golden Eggs Ltd. The kids are overpaid and the business is considered a perpetual source of revenue for all. Dad or Mom finds a place for them regardless of ability or motivation.

Primogeniture Corp. Like children's allowances, salaries are ranked according to age or seniority.

Prove Your Worth Inc. Pay is clearly based on performance, as is a secure place in the business. Unfortunately, esteem and status in the family are in doubt and are conditional upon earning the boss/parent's approval.

come into the business in the first place.

The consequences of all these scenarios spell disaster: fostering sibling resentment, hurting morale among other employees, and encouraging irresponsibility. There is struggle among family members over who gives more to the business, who is unappreciated, and whose compensation is the least fair. Symbolically, siblings may see their earnings as tokens of their worth to their parents.

Consultants dispute many issues, but they tend to agree on one thing: owners should pay family members just what they'd have to pay anyone else to perform the same job, based on the market value of that person's knowledge, talent, and experience—no more, no less.

When owners can't establish a rational compensation system for their children, openly stated and based on job performance, it is often a symptom of a company-wide problem. They haven't faced up to the need to tie compensation to performance, performance to work responsibilities, responsibilities to an overall strategic plan, and all of those things to a company work ethic.

What works best is a reward system based on productivity. It should have three components: base pay, individual productivity incentives, and participation in a shared-bonus incentive plan. Rationalizing family members' portions is a vital step toward rationalizing an entire payroll and incentive system.

It is also a vital early step in developing the next generation's owner/managers. The earnings of those who expect to own the company some day should vary directly with their own performance and with the company's performance even more than other employees.

A good sign that earnings don't have much to do with performance is when an owner or a son or daughter calls their pay a "draw." Most often, they aren't simply referring to an advance against salary. As used loosely by many owners and their family members, the word suggests drawing off water from a reservoir and thus confuses salary with profit. While our tax structure may make that "draw" advantageous in the short run (to the extent the IRS accepts the family's "draws" as salary rather than dividends), any such tax benefit is far outweighed by the company's inability to function efficiently and compete aggressively. A company simply cannot price its goods or services competitively if it is saddled with a bloated payroll.

An unrealistic salary also may cater to self-delusion regarding the "draw" to which a son or daughter is really entitled. Many a family learns too late that a relative with an addiction, say, to alcohol, drugs, or gambling, has "drawn" not only more than his reasonable compensation, but even more than the company's revenues can sustain. Even those who are potentially competent may learn to view the business as a goose that lays golden eggs—the worst possible training for them and a sure way to debilitate employee morale.

An owner who tries to solve tax and inheritance problems through salary manipulation is getting bad advice from an accountant or attorney whose vision may be limited to narrow financial considerations, and not focused on the health of the family—or, for that matter, on the welfare of the business.

Compensation and incentives for members of the family do raise important issues in connection with both the family's estate plan and the company's succession plan:

Unrealistic salaries will have made the company look more or less profitable than it really is. A fair valuation of the business must take into account either uncompensated labor or excessive "draws."

If a successor has accepted low pay because he expects to inherit a larger piece of the company than his "outside" siblings, or to purchase their stock at a discount, there had better not be any surprises later—for him or for them.

If the chosen successor's earnings are perceived as excessive by the siblings, that too may threaten his succession as well as relations among siblings and spouses.

Although all relatives' paychecks should be performance-based, the way they are formulated might be different. Suppose an owner with five children, all in their 30s, employs two of his daughters and one of his sons. With a master's degree in labor relations, Susan is personnel director. She has ambitions—when her children are older—of directing a human resources program for a much larger company or of starting her own consulting firm. Bob is a plant foreman; his personality and intellectual limitations make everyone realize that he is all but unpromotable. Karen has an engineering degree and has already worked in product design, plant management and sales, impressing her co-workers as

Getting sensible about salaries

How do you change to a rational compensation scheme based on performance and contribution when you have a tradition of "share and share alike" or of underpaying or overpaying family members?

Set a date for change. Plan to make the change with some fanfare—don't minimize it. Treat it as a significant step toward preparing the company to endure and prosper in the 21st century. Announce to all those involved that the change will take effect, say, January 1. Then have a family meeting to finalize the details.

Hear everyone out. A consultant's role in facilitating that meeting—ensuring that everyone's views are heard and that the family plans just how they will review the new system periodically—may be more important than that consultant's advice about the best specific scheme.

Be consistent and clear. Mid-sized companies have tried a variety of methods for determining family members' salaries, bonuses, and advance-

ment. Some make it a rule that siblings don't have firing, promoting, or salary-setting power over one another. Others set all family members' compensation annually at a family meeting. Still others refer management recommendations to a committee of outside directors. Whatever method you use, have a clear policy about family compensation, one which is consistent with your business philosophy and psychological working environment.

Don't mix money and emotions. Compensation should not be a means of distributing parental resources, nor of keeping children dependent, nor of buying their devotion to the family or the business.

Pay for performance. Every dollar of compensation and dollar in incentives paid to employees should be tied to achievement and aligned with the market value of that person's contribution.

Measure performance. Every family employee has a job description, and his performance is reviewed, in the same way as that of other employees,

at least once or twice a year.

Communicate. Even if it is too early to choose a successor, the family's estate plan is thoroughly reviewed and discussed openly by all adult children, those working in the business and those not, with respect to catastrophic contingency plans as well as long-term prospects.

Explain inequalities. Thoroughly discuss, with all siblings and their spouses, any anticipated inequalities in business ownership that may result, for instance, if employed shareholders exercise stock options or if an insured stock-purchase plan might be instituted.

If anyone isn't convinced that the plan is fair, the parents may finally have to say, "We're sorry that you don't see it as we do. Having heard all points of view, we feel it is the best way to be fair and to maximize the value of the assets we'll eventually be able to leave all of you. We hope you will someday become convinced it was fair." End of discussion.

well as her father.

Karen is the clear successor to ownership. However, she recently married and her career plans could change. Dad is only 57 and imagines Karen as chief executive officer in about 15 years, himself as chairman for life.

Dad is right not to give the company's stock to any of his five children. But while Susan is on straight salary and Bob's tenure with the company qualifies him for profit-sharing, Karen's compensation could include stock options or shares to be purchased back by the company if she leaves, and/or quarterly bonuses based on company performance. Her base salary might be less than she could earn elsewhere, while the total package, when she thinks of herself as an owner, is greater.

Karen's father would thus begin early to prepare her for eventual leadership and ownership. Making her earn the stock shares, rather than giving them to her, keeps his alternatives open, and puts the differential treatment of five children on a rational basis.

Business succession planners distinguish between "sweat equity" (the wealth that is built up by family members in the business) and "blood equity" (all children's fair shares of the parents' estate). The growth of shareholder value is often ignored when setting a salary. Should cumulative past compensation received by Susan, Bob, and Karen in this case figure into the calculations of their share of the estate? No. But the eventual distribution of parental wealth won't be perceived as fair by all five children—and their spouses—if they have reason to quibble over their different earnings from the business in the past. The only way to hold the estate plan and the compensation plan separate is to compensate children according to their contribution. Compensation received by relatives working in the business is bound to appear relevant to the estate plan unless everyone in the family, including spouses, agrees that family members who are working in the business have been neither overpaid nor underpaid.

A final note: There is no substitute for open communication about both compensation policies and estate planning. Enlightened owners advocate open discussion with all family members, in or out of the company, of current business involvement and compensation as well as long-term family financial matters.

— *Kenneth Kaye*

Putting extra cash in people's pockets

Some owners want to pay certain family members or employees a little extra. Here's how they do it.

Long-term incentive programs for nonfamily executives are not prevalent in family businesses. The incentive for hard work among family members is to see their controlling stockholdings increase in value. However, many family businesses fail to understand that key nonfamily managers need long-term incentives too. And if they can't get them, they'll go somewhere else.

Family employers show little interest in rewarding nonfamily members with stock. Usually the family's desire to maintain complete ownership is more important than

1. Compensation differences
Single most important way family members are favored over nonfamily employees

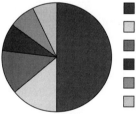

- ■ 50% Higher salary and/or bonus
- □ 14% Only ones on salary
- ■ 13% Only ones to get a bonus
- ■ 8% Special perks
- ■ 8% Salary not tied to position
- □ 7% Other

2. Noncompensation income
Single most important way family members are favored

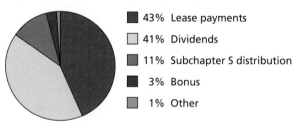

- ■ 43% Lease payments
- □ 41% Dividends
- ■ 11% Subchapter S distribution
- ■ 3% Bonus
- ■ 1% Other

3. Nonfamily owner pressure
Response to desire by nonfamily employees for ownership

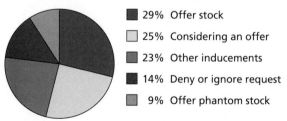

- ■ 29% Offer stock
- □ 25% Considering an offer
- ■ 23% Other inducements
- ■ 14% Deny or ignore request
- ■ 9% Offer phantom stock

Source: Towers Perrin, Philadelphia

retaining professional managers.

A 1992 survey of 450 family firms, conducted by *Family Business* magazine and Towers Perrin, a compensation consulting firm in Philadelphia, showed that family members get higher salaries and more perquisites than nonfamily members (chart 1).

The ways in which family members are favored varies. Financial planners encourage family members to own buildings or equipment and then lease them back to the company. Lease payments from the company to a family member can provide a stream of income when the individual is no longer active in the business. The survey revealed that 43 percent of the family businesses lease either a building or a piece of equipment from one or more family members (chart 2).

Other popular forms of additional income received from the business that would not normally be considered as compensation take the form of dividends or subchapter S distributions. A few other less common practices include free housing, mortgage assistance, and directors' fees.

Among the small portion of businesses that indicated there was pressure for equity ownership from nonfamily executives, 29 percent had implemented some form of stock purchase or stock option program and another 25 percent were considering some type of program, including profit sharing, higher bonuses, an ESOP, or phantom stock.

Creative ways to pay nonfamily executives

You don't have to give up ownership. A variety of "equity-emulation" techniques will attract and keep top managers.

WHEN FAMILY BUSINESSES seek to recruit a nonfamily CEO to run the company, they usually have to offer a compensation package that promises to build the individual's net worth. In the euphoria of a hiring decision, often the first thing the family gives away is equity in the business.

However, giving away equity not only dilutes family control, it can create weighty problems later on if the manager is not retained.

To hire an exceptional person, the family must be willing to provide a generous benefits package. But for the family, the nonfamily executive, and the business it is far more advantageous to find a way to emulate equity. There are a variety of equity-emulation techniques that can help

What a nonfamily manager expects

A top-level executive who's considering a position in a family firm expects much the same benefits package as he would receive in a nonfamily company. The executive will want workable answers to the following:

What happens if I get sick? Business typically answers this question with group health insurance.

What happens if I am disabled? Either group or individual policies—or both—cover long-term income replacement due to disability.

What happens if I die before retiring? Most companies have life insurance plans that provide for a fixed amount or multiple of compensation as a death benefit. Many companies also offer supplemental coverage that allows the executive to buy more protection.

Assuming I remain healthy, what will I have at the end of my tenure? The question of increased net worth may be the key to hiring the executive. Too often family firms respond by offering part of the business.

to attract and retain high-level executives. Some of these substitutes include termination agreements, supplemental executive retirement plans, pre-tax wealth accumulation plans, and private pension plans.

Termination agreements. Such agreements define compensation in the event that an executive is terminated. In addition to defining compensation, termination agreements often include vesting schedules and definitions of termination situations. Some firms base such an agreement on whether the executive had achieved certain sales and profit goals during his or her tenure. If the executive was terminated after 10 years of service, she was entitled to specific payments if the firm had achieved targets that depended on her reaching her goals and if she had remained a valuable employee. Any termination prior to 10 years reduced the payment according to a vesting schedule.

SERPs. Supplemental executive retirement plans are similar to termination agreements but most often are based on the compensation of the executive. A SERP might define what is due an executive at a specific retirement date as a percent of his final three or five years of compensation. In the event of early retirement or termination, the amount would be reduced by a formula, or vesting schedule. An example: promise an executive 60 percent of final average compensation, reduced to 40 percent for early retirement, and further reduced for termination before age 55.

Pre-tax wealth accumulation plans. Employers can set up plans that allow the executive to defer taxes on any amount of income contributed to the plan as well as on appreciation in the value of money. These plans are often used in conjunction with a supplemental retirement plan, but can be used independently as well. As an additional incentive, the company may also match the executive's contributions to the plan.

Any benefits received from a termination agreement, a supplemental retirement plan, or a pre-tax wealth accumulation plan are taxed as ordinary income at the time payments are made to the executive. Benefits may be made payable to the executive's designated beneficiary. In each of these types of plans, however, the executive becomes a general creditor of the company. In the event of an insolvency, he would have to "stand in line" with other creditors trying to get paid. If the executive is willing to be a general creditor, the benefits of these arrangements can be very attractive. On the other hand, if he is concerned about the continued viability of the business, he may look for other incentives.

All deductible (that is, tax-qualified) benefits work better for lower paid employees than for higher paid employees. Both the pre-tax wealth accumulation plan and the SERP can offset this reverse discrimination effect, which is brought about by government restrictions. Because contributions to the plan are not deductible to the company, the programs can be entirely selective; the company can set up different retirement ages and amounts for different key people.

Private pension plans. The private pension plan is similar in nature to the wealth accumulation plan and the SERP, but differs in several respects. Under the private pension plan, the executive does not become a general creditor of the company but is currently taxed on what is contributed to the plan. Thus, only the net amount after taxes accumulates for the executive's future use or retirement. The appreciation in value is not taxed, however, and the executive receives the benefits tax-free when he collects the money.

— *Alec Berkman*

Designing a phantom stock plan

The increasingly popular plans allow you to give your best people long-term incentives without diluting ownership.

PHANTOM STOCK is rising in use among family businesses. It enables nonfamily managers to share in the growing value of the company without actually owning any real stock. Phantom it may be, but its benefits are real; by the time he retires, a top executive can make tens of thousands of extra dollars if the company continues on its present growth curve. A phantom stock plan is a contract between a company and an employee. The company promises to pay the employee a sum equal to the rise in value of a hypothetical amount of company stock over a specified period of time.

Say, for example, that you assign a key vice-president 1,000 units of phantom stock in your company, valued at the time of issue at $30 per share. The price of the shares would track that of the real ones. In five years, the vice-president would receive a cash payout equal to the increase in value of his phantom shares; if the stock was worth $50 a share, he would receive the difference—$20,000—for a job well done.

The beauty of the plan is that the executive now has a personal stake in the company's growth, yet poses no threat to the family as a minority shareholder of real stock. And because the Internal Revenue Service treats the payout as regular compensation, the company can deduct the cash award when it is paid.

The challenge, though, is this: you must come up with the cash to pay the executive in five years. If you don't put money aside in a reserve fund each year or come up with another plan, you could face a serious cash flow problem when it's time for the executive to collect.

The use of phantom stock is not widespread, but it is a growing. Before going ahead with a plan, families should consider several questions.

Which employees should be included? Because phantom stock is meant to be a long-term incentive, it should be used sparingly, and should be given only to the top few employees of a company, says Ross Nager, worldwide director of family wealth planning for Arthur Andersen. The IRS considers phantom stock arrangements to be "nonqualified" plans, and, therefore, no discrimination rules apply, Nager says. The chosen employees should be in a position to have a meaningful impact on the company's future growth.

Companies have devised various ways to tie performance to reward. If there are three major divisions of a company, for example, the manager of each would receive stock according to the performance of his or her division, instead of the overall performance of the company.

How many shares should be given? The number is up to the discretion of the business owner. Often, there is a vesting schedule. If an employee leaves before the end of four years, he gets no shares. If he stays at least that long, he may earn one-third of the shares each year for the next three years. Additional shares may be granted anytime, perhaps upon promotion, or in lieu of a salary increase.

Many companies choose not to pay until the employee retires or leaves the company. A well-defined compensation package should have short-, medium-, and long-term provisions, Nager says. He suggests bonuses tied to concrete objectives for the short term, a salary and benefits plan for the medium haul, and phantom stock for the long run. Just the same, some companies are starting to pay on phantom stock every five years, so executives don't get frustrated waiting for the benefits.

How will the value of the shares be determined? The stock price often is based on the company's book value, or on a multiple of earnings. Alternatively, families can rely on a valuation of the company made by an outside appraiser. A routine appraisal of a company worth $5 million might cost from $5,000 to $10,000, though, so families may want to have an initial appraisal done and then use the appraiser's formula themselves in future years.

The phantom stock contract makes the employee a general creditor of the company. Once vested, an employee is owed the money, even if he quits on hostile terms.

How will the business come up with the cash to make the payments? Most companies create a cash reserve and contribute to it at a rate commensurate with the increase in the stock's value. Funding for the reserve should be made an annual budget item. If some of the payment is to occur

The basic plan

A typical phantom stock agreement contains the following provisions:

Start and termination dates. When the shares are given (and how many), and when they will be redeemed, typically at retirement, death, or end of employment.

Payout schedule. The intervals at which the stock will be reevaluated, and payment made. Often, firms set up a vesting schedule and make payments every five years.

Valuation. How the shares will be valued (usually based on book value or a multiple of earnings), and who will do it.

Designation of beneficiary. As in most fiduciary contracts, beneficiaries should be named.

In addition, the contract should note that the phantom shares cannot be transferred to another party. And the contract should be made binding on anyone who might buy the company.

---

at the employee's death, the company can take out life insurance to fund that portion of the claim. Also, if the plan is linked to retirement, the employee may take payment over several years, lessening the cash strain on the company.

Family business owners should consider other factors before adopting a phantom stock plan. Managers who are not included may feel slighted, and it should be made clear to them whether they'll ever have a shot at phantom stock, too.

If dividends are declared on real stock, owners should consider whether they want to make a cash award to phantom stockholders as well. And though an employee would not incur any liability if the stock decreased in value, some provision might be made to counter a decrease, especially if the employee had performed well during that time.

— *Mark Fischetti*

— IV —

OPERATIONS

◆

MUCH OF THE "HOW-TO" ADVICE in management books applies uniformly to any company, whether family owned or not. However, there are certain operational matters which require extra care in family businesses, or which can create competitive advantage. These are addressed in this section.

A particularly difficult issue is accounting; many family firms have lax practices, keep incomplete records, or hide financial information because the family can derive some benefit. Chapter 13 explains the dangers of these practices, and the payoff of keeping clean books.

Great customer service is the battle cry of the 1990s. Family companies have an inherent ability to do it better. Chapter 14 tells how.

Many family businesses define their marketing by the products they make or customers they serve. Chapter 15 explains how to escape this comfortable trap and become market driven, instead of market dependent. Families also have a unique advertising tool: The family name. It can create an edge—if ads convey the right message. Chapter 16 presents family ads that work and those that don't.

Family firms also have inherent advantages—and disadvantages —in raising capital and receiving a favorable business valuation. Chapters 17 and 18 address these matters. Finding out what competitors are up to is the focus of Chapter 19, which shows there are many low-cost techniques for scrutinizing competitors.

Finally, all good organizations must renew themselves, and the best do so before problems arise. Reengineering any firm is difficult, but it entails particular challenges—and rewards—for family companies. Chapter 20 explains how to make a successful transformation.

Accounting

How to control the bottom line

Family firms with lax or secretive accounting practices can lose track of costs and profit margins—and even encourage fraud. To avoid resulting disaster, you should divide responsibilities and share the right information.

ACCOUNTANTS SAY family operations often lack the rigid financial controls other companies employ. Even when they don't lead to fraud, lax procedures can take a harsh toll. Often family owners have poor cost-control procedures, which prevents quick corrective actions when costs are out of line, and creates difficulty in measuring profit margins and determining whether costs must be cut. An excessive emphasis on tax savings leads to counterproductive behavior like reluctance to move out inventory. Secrecy keeps employees from properly performing their jobs, or finding ways to make operations more efficient; it's also a turn-off to top outsiders whom an owner might want to hire. And if the family ever decides to sell the business, potential buyers will be turned away by an operation whose books seem questionable.

Of course, not all family businesses suffer from these ills. But many do lack "profit discipline" because they are often forced to choose between competing goals. For example, a family might prefer spending on a community project rather than on a new computer system. Or, it might overpay an incompetent relative. Owners also tend to concentrate on product quality, plant improvement, civic affairs, empire building, and personal relations to excess, beyond what these measures contribute to the long-term profits of the company.

Some of the most common pitfalls that plague the financial controls of family companies, and expert advice on how to avoid them, are presented below.

Too many family owners succumb to temptation. They deliberately keep financial controls loose in an effort to short-change Uncle Sam. Having labored long years to build up their operations, they resent having to share their rewards with a government that they see as wasteful.

Owners commonly use business checking accounts to pay for personal items. That inflates expenses and shrinks taxable income. Some families even put nannies on the company payroll. Businesses have been known to list yachts and antique cars as transportation expenses. Such creative calculations may enable a family to live lavishly without paying much of a tax tab. But sloppy accounting has its hazards—even if the owners never get caught.

To begin with, it's hard to monitor the business when expenses have been inflated. Say the average profit margin in the industry is 20 percent, and the tax-avoiding company's margin is 15 percent. It's hard to know whether the company is inefficient or if the profits only appear low because of the inflated expenses. Cooked books also complicate any relations the company may seek with outsiders. Bank loan officers take a dim view of low profits—especially if they have been held down artificially. And if the family ever decides to sell, the aggressive tax avoidance may reduce the price the company commands.

Lower profits can make it difficult to hire outside employees, too. Say the company needs to recruit one of the top salesmen in the industry. Family members may have a hard time persuading the star to leave his employer for a chance to join a company that barely shows a profit.

No matter why it's done, tax cheating also leaves a family open to blackmail. A disgruntled nonfamily employee, or an unhappy minority shareholder, could blow the whistle. Angry spouses engulfed in divorce cases have been known to declare in court that their in-laws have been hiding income. Such testimony finds its way back to the IRS.

Donald Jonovic, president of Family Business Management Services in Cleveland, says families can become addicted to using their companies as tax dodges. He urges owners to keep their books as clean as possible. Families should view tax time as an opportunity to fine tune their companies, Jonovic suggests. Their accountants should take the occasion to examine financial control systems.

An experienced accountant can offer suggestions on how to stop employee theft and manage inventory, for example. Many owners never think to ask accountants for such advice, and accountants may be reluctant to suggest that their clients should worry about being cheated.

An accountant can help the family develop a monthly budget for the business, too, and analyze problems when revenues or expenses fail to match projections. One area in which an accountant can be particularly useful is in inventory control. Jonovic says few family businesses have top-notch inventory management systems. They order too much, and allow supplies to sit around for years after they have lost value. Some companies don't even assign someone to keep track of shipments from suppliers. They rely on truck drivers to leave the proper amount.

Although the inventory accounting system should be designed with taxes in mind, tax considerations should not blind owners to larger considerations. For example, some families minimize taxes by claiming an excessively low value for inventories. That exercise can become particularly destructive if the family starts believing its own numbers and winds up with more supplies than it needs.

An accountant also can help the company develop a plan for sharing financial data with key employees. Too often family members insist on keeping data secret from everybody, even from those who need to know the numbers. One president of a distributor with revenues of $100 million kept department heads in the dark about how their units were performing. As a consequence, the president faced a huge burden he never delegated. As the only one in the company who knew what costs really were, he had to judge for himself when expenses were out of line. If he told his managers some of the numbers, they might have been able to suggest ways to cut costs.

To be sure, there may be a good reason for hiding some data. Say the company is earning huge profits from a new product. Then it would be well-advised to avoid notifying potential competitors about the gold mine. But more often, key managers should have a clear idea about the company's profits and losses. If family members are reluctant to share net profit figures, they should at least work with their accountants to develop statements of operating profits that can be relayed to managers.

Keep clean books to determine if the company is efficient. Divide tasks to prevent theft.

Many family business owners have been careful not to reveal anything about their own salaries. They may be embarrassed to admit that their take is so high—or so low. While such reticence may seem natural, consultants say key employees should be informed about all phases of company finances, including salaries.

That is particularly important if you have hired an outsider to take a key position and eventually succeed the chief executive. If you want that individual to become an effective leader, he has to appreciate everything that's going on. Unless he has access to the numbers, he won't feel he has a stake in the company. Fears that the outside executive will demand a higher salary may be unfounded. A sophisticated businessman should understand that the family's high incomes represent owners' profits, not just salaries.

At the same time, owners often put too much trust in employees. Lax financial controls go a long way toward encouraging employee theft. Loose controls also permit well-intentioned employees to run far afield. After serving a family business for years, one bookkeeper cared more about the health of the family patriarch than the patriarch's profits. When the business was struggling, she decided not to trouble the old man with bills. Instead, she tucked them away. The unpaid bills mounted and nearly bankrupted the company before the owners discovered the debts.

To avoid such problems, follow the classic advice financial textbooks preach: No matter how trusted the employee, the tasks of bookkeeping should be divided so that one person can't control the flow of money into and out of the company. If a clerk mails out checks, someone else should receive canceled checks and make sure bank accounts balance. Someone who makes purchases shouldn't be able to sign checks.

The bottom line is to keep records as true as possible. If you insist on giving family members rich perks, or cutting corners, your business won't necessarily go down the drain. But you should talk about what you are doing and be clear about why you're doing it. Otherwise things can get out of control quickly, and you'll wind up with the sort of disputes that tear businesses apart.

— *Stan Luxenberg*

Customer Service

How to do it better than competitors

By exploiting their name, values, and willingness to trust employees, family companies can provide the best service in their industry.

THE CATALOG COLOSSUS of Freeport, Maine, L.L. Bean, has long been famous for its service reps' punctiliousness and near-perfection in filling customer orders. "Sell good merchandise at a reasonable profit, and treat your customers like human beings, and they'll always come back for more," was founder Leon Leonwood Bean's Golden Rule, and it is faithfully followed today in the company led by Bean's grandson, Leon Gorman. Likewise, the public statements of other large enterprises such as Wal-Mart and Levi Strauss—even Ford, which still has family members in management and on its board—often talk about their family values.

The company that probably has the most enviable customer-service policies in America today—and certainly the best publicized—is Nordstom of Seattle. Over the past decade, sales at Nordstrom's 60 department and discount stores have grown more than sixfold, and many attribute that surge to Nordstrom's commitment to paying almost any price in order to satisfy the customer.

Nordstrom takes pride in an organization chart that is an inverted pyramid, with the customers at the top, the sales people right under them, then buyers, department managers, and store managers beneath them, and so on. On the bottom is the five-man committee that runs Nordstrom: brothers John and Jim Nordstrom, grandsons of the founder, their cousin Bruce Nordstrom; a cousin-in-law, John McMillan, and an old family friend, Bob Bender.

The bottoms-up structure is typical of the Nordstrom's approach, which exhorts front-line employees to use their own judgment in dealing with customers and calls on higher ups (or lower downs) to practice humility. When they were young, Mr. John, Mr. Jim, and Mr. Bruce, as they are known in the company, started as stock boys in what was then a chain of shoe stores. They were raised kneeling in front of the customer, says Bruce Nordstrom. The Nordstroms rely heavily on training to instill their customer-first philosophy, but they also strive to hire people with good values that are genuinely interested in helping others.

Little hard evidence exists that family owned or family controlled companies offer superior service, compared with nonfamily businesses, but one survey of smaller businesses pinpointed some differences.

Amy Lyman, a lecturer in applied behavioral science at the University of California, Davis, conducted telephone interviews with 78 business owners in Davis, a university town of 43,000 people with only one other major employer, a Beatrice/Hunt-Wesson tomato processing plant. Lyman confined her sample to businesses that sell a product, and most of the respondents were store owners with five or so employees. When she couldn't get the owner on the phone, she talked to the manager. Of the 78 people interviewed, 48 were in family owned enterprises and 30 in nonfamily enterprises.

Lyman's conclusions support the widespread belief that the personal values of the owner heavily influence the level of customer service in family firms. The heads of family firms were much more likely to say that their customer service policies reflected on them personally (51 percent versus 18 percent) and not just on the business. More of them said their policies reflected the personal family values of their childhood.

By contrast, when asked about the benefits of their customer service policies, nonfamily owners and managers were much more likely to talk about them only in financial terms. What struck Lyman most was how rarely they mentioned any link between their own values and service to the customer. They almost seemed to deny any connection.

Almost everyone interviewed said their businesses had customer service policies with which employees were expected to be familiar. But nonfamily firms were more likely to have formal, written policies. More family owners seemed to rely on informal policies that were flexible enough to allow employees' personal feelings to enter the transaction, saying, in effect, "We have rules, but if the rules don't work, then we figure out a way to meet the customer halfway." Indeed, they seemed to feel that a happy customer was one of the rewards of working in the business. Nonfamily owners and managers put more emphasis on written policies as a means of guiding and controlling employees' behavior.

The most striking finding of this small study was that the majority of family owners tended to trust their employees, while many nonfamily owners did not. Perhaps the fact that there are written rules in nonfamily firms reflected this distrust.

Most of the new wisdom on customer service stresses the importance of giving frontline employees the responsibility and authority to make decisions on such issues as customer returns or requests for repairs. What irks many customers are bland, bureaucratic replies like, "It's against the rules," or, "I'll have to ask my supervisor."

When it comes to returns of merchandise, for example, some companies like Nordstrom simply replace the item or give the customer a refund, no questions asked. The calculation here is that the loss of a customer can be far more costly in the long run than the refund.

The frustration of being hemmed in by all sorts of rules and procedures when dealing with customers was clear when Lyman surveyed employee attitudes toward service in the same firms. A typical employee of a nonfamily business reported that she "would love to be able

Being nice isn't enough. Keep up with the times, exploit new technologies, and reward employees for quality service.

to do things to satisfy the customer, but headquarters says 'No, we have to follow the rules.'"

Conflicts often arise when the manager or employee feels the customer is being dishonest—for example, lying about the condition of the product when he bought it—and yet doesn't want to lose the person's business. Some 36 percent of the respondents in family businesses said they would not compromise their values in such situations, versus 18 percent in nonfamily businesses. One respondent from a family company commented: "When you can tell the customer is lying, tell him not to come back."

The very values that cause family business owners to treat customers better may, paradoxically, make them more willing to take a stand against unreasonable or dishonest requests. Lyman believes this issue suggests the importance of boundaries in transactions with customers. You should do whatever you can to please, but there are limits.

While too many rules lead to rigid, bureaucratic responses, lack of a clear idea of what the rules are can also hamstring employees. Lyman suspects that some of the family business owners she talked to carried around their customer service policies in their heads and did not spend enough time communicating them to employees.

In larger companies, employers cannot know all their employees and whether or not their judgment can be trusted. Written policies inform employees of what is expected of them.

Some also argue that institutionalizing service policies assures consistency in dealing with customers. Studies by Benjamin Schneider, an industrial and organiza-

---

Five principles of distinctive service

In his book *The Service Edge*, business consultant Ron Zemke describes 101 firms that deliver superior service. From his study, he has distilled five principles these companies share:

1. They listen to, understand, and respond—often in unique and creative ways—to the evolving needs and constantly shifting expectations of their customers.

2. They establish a clear vision of what superior service is, communicate

that vision to employees at every level, and ensure that service quality is personally and positively important to everyone in the organization.

3. They establish concrete standards of service quality and regularly measure themselves against those standards, not uncommonly guarding against the "acceptable-error" mindset by establishing as their goal 100 percent performance.

4. They hire good people, train

them carefully and extensively so they have the knowledge and skills needed to achieve the service standards, then empower them to work on behalf of customers, whether inside or outside the organization.

5. They recognize and reward service accomlishments, sometimes individually, sometimes as a group effort, in particular celebrating the successes of employees who go "one step beyond" for their customers.

tional psychologist at the University of Maryland, College Park, underscore the point. Schneider surveyed employees' perceptions of service policies at bank branches in a populous metropolitan area and in a rural-suburban area of the Northeast. Then he asked customers of the various branches to rate the service they received.

Not surprisingly, when management had clearly defined policies that supported and rewarded employees for quality service, customers reported receiving it. Schneider says that inconsistent management policy undermined service at some banks. If employees saw that the people who were delivering the best service didn't get promoted, didn't receive the rewards, they became cynical. Employees in the same facility may be told to treat people with bigger accounts better than people with smaller accounts. They hate to do that. Customers hate it, too. That combination can be a real killer.

Schneider thinks that one of the common failings of family businesses is reliance on good-hearted motives and being nice. You can't only be nice. You have to pay attention to the details required to deliver excellent service. That includes keeping up with the times, becoming familiar with new technologies.

Call it intuition, call it instinct, but the caring of families counts heavily with customers. A can of peas is a can of peas on anybody's shelf. The difference is how the customers feel about the place while they're buying those peas.

—Howard Muson

Marketing

How to increase profit by becoming market-driven

The first step is defining the business you are really in, based on supply-side competencies and demand-side realities. Then you can craft a smart marketing plan.

ASK SENIOR MANAGERS of many family businesses about their firm's marketing, and they are likely to tell you about their hustling, aggressive sales force. Or they may try to convince you that marketing planning is something that large corporations do but is not necessary for small or medium-sized businesses. Or they may complain about wasteful expenditures on advertising.

As family businesses begin to grow, they have to change the way they identify and respond to customer needs. Instead of relying on the founder's intuitive vision, they must adopt the generic tools of market analysis and planning. Instead of focusing all their efforts on pushing products out the door, they have to analyze marketing trends in order to understand changing customer needs and desires. Otherwise, they may wake up one day and find they are still pushing products but no one is buying them.

Although many family firms talk about good marketing, their true orientation is quite different from that of the best market-driven companies. Four lingering beliefs prevent family companies from adopting and maintaining a systematic marketing orientation, which makes them vulnerable to the shifting currents of demand.

1. The belief that the founder's vision will ensure success forever. Owners of family businesses often believe that their success is the best evidence of their marketing prowess. The problem with that attitude is that as markets change, the founder's vision may no longer assure success.

By the same token, successors to the business often believe that they must demonstrate the same kind of intuitive genius that led the founder to create the business. Though they frequently enter the business via sales, some successors make little effort to learn what it takes to do effective marketing. They may never get around to setting up a formal mechanism for marketing planning.

Unfortunately, marketing vision is not always promoted in the gene pool. Family successors spend most of their time either trying to carry on the business in the mold established by the founder, or by imposing their own ideas for internal change. Meanwhile, the company may be caught off-guard as shifts develop in the marketplace.

2. The belief that marketing is advertising, selling, and personal relationships. A family company may have a marketing manager or even a marketing department, but the role assigned to both is largely promoting the firm's products or services. The company may use advertising, while grumbling about whether it is really effective. The sales force may hold planning meetings that are really cheerleading sessions to exhort them to greater effort. And much emphasis is placed on what one expert calls the "lunch-golf-dinner" model of marketing.

No one would deny that personal relationships are important in business, and marketing does indeed emphasize the selling function. But the best marketing firms understand these activities to be part of a much larger strategy that is aimed at sensing and satisfying customer needs.

3. The belief that "We really know our customers." This belief is an outgrowth of the wrong-headed notions that marketing is selling and is based on cultivating personal relationships. Some family firms may organize a few focus groups to assess what their customers like or dislike. But many rely on what they feel is an instinctive knowledge of their customers rather than a well-developed research base.

In contrast, market-driven firms conduct systematic, ongoing research into the needs of their customers and the broader market. They know with much greater precision the desires of their potential customer base—and in their planning they constantly look for new trends and niches that they can serve.

4. The owner's belief that someone else is supposed to "do" marketing. As family businesses grow, the owner-manager may appoint someone to be the marketing manager. The CEO assumes that this person will do at least a competent marketing job. There are two problems with this.

First, in a privately held firm, the marketing manager can, consciously or not, begin to feel that the CEO is the customer. Rather than seeking ways to satisfy the ultimate consumer's needs and wants, the manager attempts to satisfy what he perceives to be the CEO's needs and desires.

Second, while it makes good sense to delegate some specific marketing functions, firms that are truly marketing-driven take Tom Peters' advice: Everyone does marketing. This means that the CEO has to take the lead in establishing a culture that is focused on good marketing. In such a culture, marketing is not just one business function. The satisfaction of customer needs becomes the starting point for all the firm's activities, for decisions on product, price, promotion, and distribution.

Steps to becoming market driven. The two hemispheres of business activity are the "supply side" and the "demand side." The supply side consists of all the internal activities and outputs that generate revenue for the firm. The demand side consists of all the uncontrollable forces that shape the magnitude and nature of sales results.

Rank the kinds of customers that can be served. Then satisfy each group's needs.

Business people make supply-side decisions based on their understanding of demand-side forces. In family businesses, however, their understanding is often shaped by the founder's vision. In addition, they are naturally more comfortable on the supply side: holding meetings, dictating correspondence, dealing with subordinates, and making decisions at the office or plant.

The demand side, in contrast, is an inherently threatening place. Consumers rarely tell you exactly what they are thinking, because they don't know themselves. Competitors are even more furtive and unpredictable. New technologies, new government regulations, and a host of other uncontrollable forces can often disrupt a company's plans.

If business owners allow it to, the supply side will consume most of their time and energy. Many of them complain that running the day-to-day business and fighting fires leaves little or no time to engage in systematic planning. Perhaps because of this very stress these owners sometimes prefer to spend their time on activities which are under their relative control—the production of the goods and services that have always produced their revenue—rather than on trying to understand the messy world outside.

The first step to becoming market-driven is to ask

yourself what business you are really in. Most small companies answer the question by listing the products they make or the services they offer—for example, "We're in the landscaping business."

That definition distinguishes the company from, say, a sausage maker, but it is too general to be illuminating. Are they talking about residential or commercial landscaping? Do they mean planning and developing landscapes or just grounds maintenance? Is the business going after cost-conscious customers or customers who are more interested in quality?

The definition of the business should reflect supply-side competencies as well as demand-side realities. If other companies have greater experience and acknowledged skills at designing and creating residential landscapes it may be best to leave that segment to the competitors.

The process of defining the business means picking and choosing among market segments. It is not enough, for example, to define the market as "all the businesses in my geographic area." Market-driven companies select and rank-order the kinds of customers they wish to serve. These customers usually represent market niches that the company believes it can dominate.

The outcome of this "business-definition exercise" should be a clear vision of the products and services that the business wishes to offer, and an equally clear vision of the markets and businesses that it most wishes to serve.

The second step is to come up with a marketing plan. Often, family companies that claim to have a plan for the next year have little more than a series of financial projections—simple extrapolations of how much more business they expect to do next year compared with this year.

These are not plans at all. They are merely hopes built on guesswork rather than systematically projected numbers. Marketing plans don't have to be thick volumes of facts and figures; those kinds of plans usually get put on a shelf and are never read. The primary criterion for a good marketing plan is whether it is used on a regular basis for making decisions. A marketing plan simply answers three questions:

1. Where are we now? This is stock-taking. Beyond knowing what a firm's sales volumes are, managers should be able to articulate the company's position in various market segments and to provide quantitative information on those positions (costs, sales, growth trends, and so on). To analyze these segments properly, managers should understand how the company stacks up against competitors in each of them. Supply-side information is also required: What is the state of the company's plants compared with those of its competitors? How does product quality compare? To provide the most useful basis for planning, the information should be organized by market segment.

2. Where do we want to go? To answer this question, managers must first create goals, which are broad statements of desired ends, then set objectives, which are desired near-term results that can be measured. Some business decisions will be designed to achieve near-term results, others will be aimed at accomplishing more distant payoffs. For example, one goal of the landscape company might be "to dominate landscape maintenance services in planned communities of over 300 acres in 10 states." The objective to support that goal might be "to increase sales in this segment by 10 percent in the next 12 months."

The business may set other kinds of goals as well. For example, as a basis for future planning, management may state its intentions to investigate specific new markets or product opportunities.

3. How do we get there? Management actions will be geared to achieving both short-term and long-term results. For example, to reach new customers in planned communities with over 300 acres, the company may have to hire a new type of sales manager to identify and make contact with companies in this market segment. To achieve longer-range objectives, the company may want to initiate a study of the market potential for all of its services in states where it is not currently operating.

Businesses will remain successful as long as they satisfy customer needs and do so in a way that is profitable and is better than that of the competition. But in today's intensely competitive environment, success requires more than hard work, intensive activity, and a casual, seat-of-the-pants approach to marketing. Family businesses delude themselves when they believe that they are different from large public companies and do not have to use the tools of modern marketing analysis and planning. The result is complacency, and a reactive posture rather than a proactive one.

Firms that do not institutionalize planning may have a myopic view of the marketplace that leads to decline and, ultimately, extinction. Low production costs, average quality, and a sound balance sheet no longer assure a company of success. Companies that define their business in terms of customer needs—and gear all their operations to satisfying that need better than their competitors—will be winners in the 1990s.

— *Scott Ward*

Advertising

How to benefit from your family name

Promoting the family can give your company a strong edge on competitors—if your advertisements convey the right message. Ads that work and ads that don't.

THERE'S NO MISTAKING that Daw's Home Furnishings in El Paso, Texas, is a family business. The store's full-page ads in local newspapers proclaim "Home Owned and Operated for Over 38 Years!" The smiling mugs of eight members of "the Daw Gang" look out from the listings of weekly specials on items such as frost-free refrigerators, microwave ovens, and mattresses. Each photo has a caption with the family member's name and number of years in the business ("Linda Daw Hudson, 19 years of experience"). Just in case anyone has missed the point, a small map of Texas in the upper right-hand corner is accompanied by the legend: "We're from El Paso!...We live, bank, and spend here! We buy, hire, and like it here! We've been here 38 Years."

Although more emphatic about it than most, the Daws are not alone in touting their company's family ties. Through the years, many others, small and large, have designed their marketing strategies around a family theme, often memorably.

Older television viewers in the New York City metropolitan region will remember the Castro Convertible commercials back in the late 1940s and early 1950s, in which little Bernadette Castro opened her father's convertible beds and showed how easy it was. Bernadette is now president of the company and her children appear in commercials nationwide.

The selling of the family is an old and hallowed marketing strategy that may enjoy a resurgence now that family values are back in style. From small businesses that advertise locally to large companies trying to reach a national audience or segmented markets, such as Columbia Sportswear in Portland, Oregon, the family pitch is still common.

Using the family in advertising the business has its risks.

Does it really work? The answer seems to be, "It depends." According to those who have tried it, putting the family out front can distinguish a small company, or one that is new to a given industry, from giant, well-entrenched competitors. It can help to convey, convincingly, a concern for quality and integrity. By making customers feel they know the people behind the product, it can endow the company and the product with a strong personal image.

But promoting the family may be more appropriate in certain industries and market segments than in others. To some people, the family owned company still carries a stigma of amateurish management and nepotism.

Hard evidence is lacking on the question of whether a family-centered ad campaign works. That's because most family businesses are too small, or simply too busy, to do the kind of detailed market research that huge corporations routinely use to gauge customers' reactions to advertising.

It's difficult to quantify the dollars-and-cents impact of a family's celebrity. But one clue to a campaign's success may be a company's growth. Sales have increased dramatically since the Daws started promoting the family nature of their store.

A similar, if somewhat more subdued, marketing strategy has helped Redmond Products, a Minnesota company that sells Australian hair care products. The company's ads in national magazines feature photographs of seven family members involved in the business. One memorable ad showed the whole three-generation clan, including toddlers, dressed up in kangaroo costumes—a spoof of the company's kangaroo logo.

Tom Redmond Sr., who started the company in 1980 with his daughter Patricia, says when you're a small company competing against Revlon, Proctor & Gamble, and Colgate-Palmolive, you can't outmuscle or out-advertise them. If you mimic their marketing, they'll eat your lunch. So you have to do what they can't do.

Redmond also believes that the family-oriented strategy creates an honest, credible image. He feels women who buy shampoo for their families identify more readily with someone else's family than with a glamorous model or actress.

What's more, he believes consumers trust a family company not to deceive them. Nobody raises their kids teaching them to lie, cheat, and steal. So certain values are likely to be ingrained that have to do with what kind of citizens you want your kids to be. If your advertising focuses on that, your customers pick up on it and respect it.

If a family-centered campaign can build trust with customers, it can also identify the product with a particularly vivid personality. Columbia Sportswear, the large manufacturer of upscale ski parkas and other outdoor gear in Portland, Oregon, provides an outstanding example.

In Columbia's ads, Gert Boyle, the chairwoman, is portrayed as a dour, overbearing, perfectionist mother who is a constant—and comical—trial to her son, Tim, the company president. However, the message conveyed is that Mom imposes tough quality standards that Tim constantly struggles to meet—that is, that Columbia Sportswear gear is better than the rest.

The Boyles credit the ongoing campaign with playing a critical role in Columbia's remarkable turnaround. Just 15 years ago, the company was barely making ends meet. Since the campaign, revenue has skyrocketed. Most of that growth has been in the nine years since bossy Mother Boyle has dominated advertising. The firm's previous ads were "pseudo-techie"—emphasizing, for instance, the scientific reasons that Columbia clothing keeps customers warmer than competing products. But the mother-and-son ads get attention as well as make a point. You can have the greatest product in the world, but it won't sell if your ads are so boring that no one notices them.

Some companies have figured out that a family pitch connects with certain audiences even more than others. Marcal Paper Mills, a maker of household paper goods, has tailored its image to appeal to two distinct market segments in the northeastern United States: supermarket owners and Hispanics.

In the supermarket trade press and other advertising to vendors, Marcal emphasizes that the company has been family owned and operated for three generations. Supermarkets that stock Marcal products identify with family ownership for the simple reason that many of them are multigeneration family companies, too.

Likewise, research reveals that Hispanic shoppers respond even more warmly to the family connection than do "Anglos." Thus, marketing aimed at flourishing Hispanic communities in the Northeast uses the slogan: "Calidad que va de familia a familia"—which translates roughly, "Quality from our family to your family." And some of the most loyal customers overlap the two market segments: grocery stores and other small businesses run by Hispanics.

Although advertising the family may seem as innocent and harmless as mom and apple pie, there are reasons for proceeding with caution. When you and your family are out there in the public eye, as the owners of a prosperous business, there can be security problems. Particularly for families with young children, the worry of kidnap may outweigh any potential gain.

There are also strong business reasons why some companies do not want to emphasize family ownership. The business that aspires to become a high-tech, global

Does your family have the right stuff?

You don't want to put your family in your ads just for the fun of it. If you don't think about how it can help the company image, the strategy may not work.

Corporations take on many human characteristics in the minds of their employees and customers. A company may be thought of as honest, friendly, trustworthy, and very demanding in its standards of quality and service. Or, unfortunately, it may be thought of as cold, sloppy, nondescript, or even untrustworthy.

The family can personify some of the company's most appealing traits. But before deciding whether to use your family in your advertising, you should first examine the qualities customers look for in your product category.

Do they base their buying decisions mostly on attributes of the product, such as usefulness, style, color, or prestige value? If so, an advertising strategy that focuses on the family can get in the way of selling the product.

In some categories, however, attributes of the company are the biggest influence on the buyer's choice. For example, insurance companies, banks, brokerages, and other financial institutions often spend more on corporate image advertising than on product advertising. After all, money is a commodity; what distinguishes one source of money from another is the institution behind it.

In selling a company image, four of the most important attributes are trustworthiness, credibility, service, and quality. These features can be very effectively personified by the family.

Don't take the family approach just as a way to tie a campaign of ads together, however. The family is no substitute for a message. And don't use family members unless their personal characteristics somehow express qualities of the product or the company that you want to emphasize in your message. —*Tom Garbett* company may want to keep its family origins in the background. If you're building jet engines, the cozy little family workshop is not exactly the best image for you to convey. Image-makers frequently cite IBM and Ford as examples of global leviathans that, at least in recent years, have played down their family roots.

Using the family does not, by itself, ensure the success of an ad campaign. By picturing themselves in their ads, the Daw Gang identifies the family with the business. But effective advertising can raise the visibility of the business even without the family. The family can only be a means of demonstrating your idea or selling messages. It's not a substitute for an idea, but a way of dramatizing it and making it credible. For example, Bernadette Castro was darned cute, but her appearance in the commercials was effective because it dramatized the message, which was that opening Castro convertible beds was so easy that even a child could do it.

Also, using the family in commercials may not succeed unless the members somehow personify the product.

If the family comes across as warm and friendly, that might be the right persona for a restaurant. But if you own a store that sells computers and other electronic equipment, the family members would have to come across as technical whizzes.

Whatever the message, family owned companies that play up ties to kith and kin may enjoy an advantage. According to demographers and other professional trend-spotters, the next 10 years may be the most home- and family-oriented since the 1950s. The prosperous baby boomers are coming into the most intensely home-focused stage of the life cycle (settling down, raising kids). As this huge cohort concentrates on child-rearing, marketers of every stripe will rediscover family values such as stability, integrity, quality, and a more nebulous sort of warm, fuzzy concern for people and prosperity. Slogans like "From our family to your family" are likely to pluck consumers' heartstrings for another decade.

— *Anne B. Fisher*

Raising Capital

Getting money from private sources

Private capital markets are exploding. Five experts explain what you have to do to qualify for growth or succession financing.

THERE IS PLENTY of private capital around for family companies wishing to finance succession or take a leap to the next level in size. The range of options can, in fact, be a little bewildering. Commercial banks provide working capital, and some do private placements. Many firms offer venture capital, sometimes in combination with a public offering. Others specialize in "mezzanine" financing, or subordinated debt. Smaller lenders and investment firms are popping up all over the country.

To explain how to judge these sources, and what family businesses have to do to qualify for them, *Family Business* magazine convened a panel of five experts whose firms are representative providers of long-term debt and equity financing. The experts are: Michael Carter, managing director of Carter & Co., a "boutique" investment firm in Southport, Connecticut; Dirk R. Dreux IV, director of private business advisory services at U.S. Trust in New York City; Thomas L. Kelly II, general partner of CHB Capital Partners in Denver; Harvey A. Mackler, executive vice-president of Gibralter Corp. of America, a subsidiary of UJB Financial; and Donald P. Remey, managing director of BCI Advisers Inc. in Teaneck, New Jersey.

Q. What do professional investors and advisors look for in a company seeking financing?

A. They become interested when management and the owners are passionate and 100 percent focused on building the business. If owners view their business as a job and not something that absorbs them 60 hours per week, they tend to lose interest.

When it comes to management, the first thing they look for is character. The second requirement for asset-based loans is adequate collateral. Other ingredients include owners' ability to keep the ship going right and their ability to react to different market conditions.

Furthermore, the most desirable businesses have a "defensible market niche," and are in an industry that has attractive growth or profitability characteristics.

However, investors will also work with businesses in industries that are consolidating and shrinking. They will back sensational people if their business can consistently outperform their peers in the industry, and are in the top 10 percent of their market.

Q. Are there any businesses that investors won't touch?

A. Franchise businesses, because of the short time horizons and very localized nature of the business.

Q. Do family owned firms have any special characteristics that would prevent investors from financing them?

A. Definitely. The very first step in financing is to look at the business owner's objectives. If they are not clear and focused, investors pass. If three different generations have three different sets of objectives, that is not a financable situation. The business objectives have to line up, and with two or three generations, they rarely do.

Investors also have a bit of a bias against businesses where there is a husband and wife or siblings involved. It makes a business somewhat less attractive because it reduces the control and flexibility of the owner-entrepreneur. If there is a problem, you can't fire someone as easily as you can in another business.

The family part of a family owned business can either be a great positive or a great negative. When looking at a family company, two sets of due diligence are done that are completely separate: One is on the business itself, and the other is on the family. Both of them have to come out with a clean bill of health for the investor to move forward on the deal. That is part of what makes investing in this market a little trickier.

Q. Does the due diligence include looking for a succession plan?

A. Investors look at management succession first. What is the backup management? Who is here to run this company?

Q. How is the due diligence done?

A. Most of the checks are financial and legal. Have these people been involved in any kind of financial problems, in bankruptcy? Has an owner run up over $100,000 in credit card debt and walked away from it? Has a manager been charged with sexual harassment?

The second aspect of due diligence is talking to as many people as possible about the company. Investors ask for a list of references, but that is just the starting point. They use that reference list to find out the names of other people who know the company.

One of the questions that is always asked early on is: "We are going to investigate you and your company in detail. Is there anything that, if we had unlimited time and perfect information, we will find out that you should explain before we find it?"

Q. How about asking the hard questions about relationships between husband and wife, or a father and son, or two brothers?

A. Investors are very direct about it. They ask for specific examples of where there was disagreement and how it was resolved. Sometimes they find out a lot about the way problems are handled in the business by going out with sales people or visiting with customers.

Investors also spend a great deal of time doing blind interviews with suppliers and customers of the company. Within the company, they talk to a lot of lower-level employees in addition to senior management. A simple technique is to ask different people the same question and see if the same answer is given.

Q. Private equity capital is exploding and there's been tremendous growth in the number of equity investors. Yet, at the same time, investors' cost structures make it prohibitive to do business with smaller companies. What are an owner's options?

A. Investment banking firms add significant value. By screening, packaging, and structuring financing opportunities, they "tee up" smaller transactions for institutional investors. They eliminate a significant cost for these investors and make it easy for them to come to a quick yes or a quick no.

There is a tremendous amount of capital available, but for the most part, the smaller companies don't know how to access it. They don't know how to go about seeking introductions in a professional manner. Investors are seeking high-quality transactions but are having a hard time finding them. This puts a certain type of high-qual-

ity, emerging-growth company very much in demand. There is a lot of money chasing a smaller number of transactions. But capital providers are struggling to stay within the stricter parameters that they set for themselves as a result of their experience during the crazy 1980s.

However, it's important to put the abundance of capital in perspective. At least on the equity side, the majority of capital that has been raised is not even looking at the bulk of the family business market. Studies have shown that 90 to 95 percent of closely held, family businesses have between zero and $25 million in revenues. And this new capital has all been raised to look at $50 million, $100 million, $200 million sales companies. The quality of a firm that is doing only $2 million in sales really doesn't matter; it is going to have a tough time attracting capital. Unfortunately, it's as simple as that.

On the other hand, niche private equity pools are developing. Some of the new funds that have been developed are more focused than before. So you will find funds focused on family businesses, or media properties, or some other specific niche in which they have a track record. But it is much easier to raise a $5-million than a $1-million equity placement. There should be a lot more cheering for those who can raise $1 million. There are fewer players for small transactions, but they're out there.

Smaller businesses should develop relationships with local, smaller boutiques, which can be found in every city in this country—the local boutique investment banker and financial advisor.

The smaller the business, the more important it is to have a referral that will ensure that the company gets attention from potential investors. Smaller businesses should use their advisors, their accountant or lawyer, to help them reach prospective capital sources.

The good news is that there's so much money around, and people will find it. To many entrepreneurs, however, the cost of that capital sounds outrageously expensive. More than 20 percent a year compounded for five years is not uncommon. It's a big number. And these numbers are very difficult for small businesses to generate. Yet that is the price of equity money. In fact, for smaller amounts, the cost of capital is even higher, because the investor is taking a greater risk and the transaction costs are high.

Small businesses have to be realistic about the availability of capital for them. That's the best way to start thinking about how they can ameliorate their situation.

Q. How and where should owners professionalize their companies in order to attract private capital? Where should they put most of their time and energy?

A. The first thing they should do is to surround themselves with good people. The second thing is to listen to those people.

It is also critically important to correctly motivate your key people, to work on compensation-incentive plans to ensure that the key people act like owners. Most of the time that involves giving them equity. Investors are very concerned that a key scientist or a key marketing person will leave for another $10,000 or $15,000. And for a certain type of emerging growth company, investing in a quality CFO will pay for itself in multiple ways.

Owners should also spend time developing a mission and a strategic plan, so they can articulate for investors, employees, customers, and vendors where they are taking the company and why anyone should invest in it. They have to view capital from the standpoint of a business's life cycle.

One indication of whether the entrepreneur is going to listen is whether there is a board of directors or a board of advisors already in place. Whether they will listen to a board is another question, but if they at least have one, it suggests they have realized there is some value in outside advice.

Related to that and equally important is the management succession issue. Every business has to look very carefully at its key positions and ask the question: "What happens if that person gets hit by a bus?" Smaller businesses that can't afford to have a bunch of extra people sitting around have a hard time addressing the "hit-by-the-bus issue."

You don't necessarily have to have a replacement for each manager within the business. But you should have a plan for recruiting one in an emergency. If you have anyone in the company who is considered completely irreplaceable, that is a risk factor. For an investor, it raises a red flag.

Q. A lot of people don't know what it costs to work with different types of capital providers. What are some rough estimates on pricing?

A. At the senior debt level, you are looking at an interest rate related to prime or some other floating rate, plus fees, plus some balances. In today's market that probably gets you up in the 11 percent to 12 percent area. In the mezzanine sector, which is subordinated debt, the rate tends to be in the high teens up to the low 20s. And equity capital's expectations tend to be higher than that—25 percent and higher.

It is terribly important that family businesses understand the cost of capital. The money that goes into these businesses has alternative places to go. Over the last 10 years, for example, the stock market has provided a return in excess of 15 percent. Investors don't invest

Investors will support an owner's business decisions if there has been open discussion.

unless they get competitive returns.

Often, pricing includes a retainer, a success fee, and a post-closing monthly retainer in certain situations. In general, the success fee is 1 to 2 percent for debt, 3 to 4 percent for mezzanine, and 5 to 8 percent for equity.

Others are looking for a compounded annual return of 30 percent. There is no interest rate on the investment. The investors are investing side by side with the entrepreneur or the family or the management team. Furthermore, they bring more to the table than just capital. They have expertise within their firm that a small business could not afford to have in-house, such as corporate finance and mergers and acquisition expertise, market-entry strategies, and productivity enhancements.

Q. What about the issue of control? Many business owners don't like to be told what to do. They worry that the investor will get too involved and tell them, "Joe, you really need a CFO, or you have to do this or that."

A. The further down in the capital structure the investor is, the more influence he or she is going to want to have. An equity investor in a business is really partnering with the owners and the management team. They therefore expect to have a commensurate say in the running of the business.

They are not that sensitive about having voting control. They are willing to take minority positions in closely held businesses. While they may not have voting control, however, they do expect to have input on key strategic decisions in the company. It is usually the business owners who are most open to outside advice that make the best investment candidates.

Investors not taking equity want the business to become as successful as it can be. Their degree of involvement and advice is to get the company to that goal. If the family owner views the advice as helping him or her to get to that goal and internalizes it, is that control or is that help? It is control if the owner disagrees with it.

Q. What happens if they disagree?

A. Investors and owners will disagree on certain things. What investors want from owners is healthy, open, rational discussion of the pluses and minuses of what they want to do and why they want to do it. In many discussions there is not a right and wrong answer. So at the end of the day the investor will support the owner's decision if there has been an open discussion. If the owner is wrong often enough, however, the investor will want to have some way of replacing him or her. And that is where control really becomes an issue.

Valuation

How to influence the valuation of your company

Many decisions a valuator makes are subjective. You can influence at least five of those judgements by providing select information.

THERE ARE MANY important occasions during the life of a family business when valuation of the company is needed. And almost always, at least two parties with opposing interests are typically involved in the outcome of the valuation. They might be stockholders who need a value for a buy-sell agreement. Perhaps the business is being sold, so there is a buyer and a seller. The parties may be divorcing spouses, or separating partners. Or the valuation may be for the purpose of calculating gift or estate taxes, with the government and the estate and gift beneficiaries as the principal parties.

In every business valuation, there will be a winner and a loser. You can influence the outcome—legitimately—by being ready to present the right kind of information.

The valuator must gather many facts about the business and learn about the economic environment in which it operates. The key to estimating the value of a business is learning about and understanding the economic forces that affect it—trends in its industry, its market share, wage levels, competing products, and so on. The owners are a primary source for this information. One way or another, consciously or unconsciously, the valuator will be influenced by information you provide.

Most family owned businesses are valued by some variation of the "build-up method." This method is easily portrayed with a simple equation: estimated future benefits (earnings or cash flow) divided by an appropriate rate (based on a market assessment of the risk involved in the company) equals the value of the business. To see how the formula works, here is a simple example: estimated future benefits of $2 million, divided by a rate of 33 percent, equals a value of $6 million. On the surface, this appears to be a pretty straightforward calculation—unless you consider the numerous judgements that go into arriving at both estimated future benefits and an appropriate discount or capitalization rate.

The determination of earnings begins with the company's financial statements, but business valuators almost always adjust those numbers. Even audited statements will be changed if the owners' compensation or other payments to relatives, such as rent, are considered abnormally high or low. Many types of owners' perquisites are commonly found on the books of privately owned businesses, including nonworking relatives on the payroll. Adjustments have to be made in order to "normalize" the books in such cases, so that the numbers can be compared with the numbers of other companies or with industry averages.

Some of these judgments are based on objective research, for example, on studies of compensation levels for top officers in the industry or geographic region. Others, however, are almost entirely subjective. To ensure an outcome favorable to them, business owners should find out what major adjustments the valuator plans to make and offer their input on what is normal for their industry and geographic location.

Valuators also have the option of using an alternative to the build-up method. They can rely on market data for shares in publicly traded companies or information on the sale of comparable private companies. If they choose this approach, an essential first step is finding companies with comparable financial profiles. To do so, the valuator needs to gain an in-depth understanding of the market, the competition, the industry, trade associations, factors influencing pricing decisions, what drives costs. When a company has a bunch of unrelated products or services that reflect the preferences of the founder, it is sometimes difficult to decide what industry that company is in. Whoever supplies the necessary information will be in a position to influence the outcome of the valuation. And the best source is—you guessed it—the business owner.

Many times, the valuator will not find any public companies that are similar enough to be used for comparisons. But the search for transactions between comparable private companies—the other possible yardstick—can be even trickier, since this type of information is not easily available. The business owner can thus become an important guide, referring the valuator to economists in trade associations, editors of trade publications, suppliers, competitors, and other sources who might have knowledge of such deals. It is also not uncommon for the valuator in such situations to rely heavily on information provided by the principals in the business.

If there are no comparable publicly traded companies whose stock value can be used, or private transactions in which the selling price is known, the valuator usually employs the build-up method. As indicated, this method is loaded with subjective judgments.

Few family business owners are comfortable predicting future earnings or cash flow, but that's exactly what the valuator must do in order to calculate the value of the business. How can an outsider do this when the owner, who is closest to the business, is reluctant to do it? Here again, you have an opportunity to provide information that could have a significant impact on the outcome. Put aside any squeamishness about making predictions and come up with the best (optimistic or pessimistic) estimates you can.

A key factor in such estimates is the trend of earnings in past years. If the trend has been consistent, the valuator will probably use it to project future earnings. If the trend has been inconsistent, the valuator will be inclined to predict the same inconsistency in the future—unless the owner can make a convincing case for a different scenario.

For example, a company that has traditionally sold machine tools to the automotive and aerospace industries is now selling to medical device manufacturers. The owner would want to point out to the valuator that this offers a more stable market for the future. In another case, a software developer now has a mature product that requires relatively low costs to maintain. The development costs have hurt profits in the past, but this business is justified in projecting higher profits in the future.

Don't be squeamish about estimating future earnings or cash flow.

The above points address the future benefits side of the equation. Obviously, the rate that is applied to capitalize these benefits is equally important. Much of the mystique surrounding the valuation process comes from the calculation of the rate of risk in the business being valued. Business valuation is more art than science, and much creativity goes into determining the appropriate rate.

The rate will differ according to what future benefit it will be applied to, earnings or cash flow. The rate will also vary depending on whether it is a minority interest or a controlling interest that is being valued. If the build-up method is used, the rate calculation may depend upon other factors such as the relative size of the business, the effectiveness of management, the impact of technology on process and products, the strength of the competition, the adequacy of capital to fund future growth, and so on. While experienced business valuators can make reasonable estimates of these factors, a good deal of subjectivity cannot be avoided. In all these areas, the opinions of the present owners of the business can influence the rate ultimately chosen.

An appraiser often makes subjective judgments and consults multiple sources during at least five major steps in the valuation process. The five stages are: 1. The initial visit, in which the appraiser is briefed on the business and its industry and observes the physical plant; 2. the valuator's historical analysis of operating results, adjusted for compensation and other discretionary payments to family members such as rent; 3. estimates of future performance, based in part on management's plans and anticipated changes in the competitive and economic climate; 4. the search for comparable companies and selection of criteria to be used to estimate future benefits; 5. the calculation of a capitalization or discount rate that accurately reflects the risk involved in the business.

Each of these five steps leaves room for interpretation, and those closest to the business, as providers of information, can thus legitimately influence the outcome. Of course, business owners cannot provide false or inaccurate information in order to mislead the valuator. The best valuations are performed by well trained, highly professional valuators, who are adept at spotting inflated (or deflated) numbers and crude attempts at deception.

— *Richard F. Lane*

Spying on the Competition

How to find out who's doing what

Vital information you thought was locked away—a competitor's cost of sales, production, employment—can be found with clever (and inexpensive) sleuthing.

COMPANIES HAVE ALWAYS had to keep close tabs on competitors and markets, and many family companies seem to know almost instinctively what they have to find out and where they can do it. Their CEOs go to the same trade shows as their competitors and read the same trade publications. They may even play golf with them and exchange plant visits. They have a better gut feel for what's going on inside the competitor.

Especially after the early years of success, however, many family companies may become inward-looking and complacent. They are confident they know all about the competition and don't need to know more. But as the business world spins faster on its axis—changing markets, shifting of commerce—companies need more than ever to know what competitors are doing.

Even small companies nowadays have to be more aggressive about monitoring the competition, more knowledgeable about potential sources, more sophisticated in how they analyze data. Otherwise, they may be caught asleep in their own industry Pearl Harbors.

Large companies spend anywhere from thousands to millions of dollars for intelligence research. Experts agree, however, that companies can do a lot by themselves, with small budgets and their own personnel.

For starters, someone in the company should know how to use a library and conduct a computer search. Many small companies do not scratch the surface of knowledge about their competitors and markets simply because no one is trained in how to find it.

"No company should be ignorant of the databases that exist out there today," says Leonard Fuld, whose Fuld & Co. in Cambridge, Massachusetts, performs intelligence research for companies. "It's an embarrassment if they are." Fuld recommends that small companies send one of their employees to one of the many training sessions offered on what databases are available and how to conduct searches.

The second thing corporate sleuths need to learn is not to be bashful about asking for competitive information on the phone. Leila Kight, whose Washington Researchers also conducts seminars on intelligence gathering, spends a lot of time teaching the participants how to win friends and ask shrewd questions on the telephone. "They have to be able to get on the phone and ask for help, to call on the trade association in the industry, a member of the trade press, the Department of Commerce official who covers that industry."

The good news is that your present staff is probably all you'll ever need for intelligence gathering. But you must recognize what each person can do for you and point them in the right direction.

Because they get around in the community, family members can pick up valuable leads from people who also deal with their competitors—town officials, bankers, newspaper editors, plumbers. They should be urged to pass those leads on to staff if they don't already. Aside from family members, the following employees can contribute vital information.

Marketing people. Most intelligence gathering in smaller companies is done by marketing departments, Fuld says. That's because marketing usually has people who do research, who know the most about gathering data and available sources. When a CEO wants to start up an intelligence operation he is thus likely to turn to them.

Salespeople. When talking to customers salespeople

naturally hear talk about their competitors' products and prices. Take Bell Power Systems, a family company in Connecticut that sells refurbished John Deere diesel engines for industrial and agricultural machines. Arnold Bell, the president, says his sales people regularly report on models, sizes, and service backup for the engines of his domestic and foreign competitors. Bell says, "They have learned from customers that the foreign-made engines are expensive to repair and lack spare parts"—information that's obviously useful in selling Bell's engines.

Purchasing agents. They find out a great deal from talking with suppliers and contractors who also do business with competitors. One Pennsylvania construction company, H.B. Alexander & Sons, asks its purchasing agents to write call reports that are kept on file and contain much competitor information. According to Bill Alexander, chairman of the third-generation company, purchasing agents, when sounding out, say, suppliers of structural steel for a job that is up for bid, may find out that a competitor is "really going after this project," or that "no one else has called us on the job."

Customer service reps. They often hear about the kind of service competitors are offering. For example, they may find out that a competitor has a new slogan-driven offer of guaranteed on-time delivery or free service. They may also hear about under-the-table dealing, as when competitors offer kickbacks of goods to their customer's employees. According to Christopher Ritz, a customer relations specialists with RSS Inc. in New Haven, Connecticut, companies' efforts to get their reps to file reports on competitors often falter because the reps don't want to spend the time and feel their reports aren't used. But Ritz thinks that if they can enter the information on their desktop terminals, into a database that organizes it, they'll be more wiling to do so.

R&D people. They regularly attend meetings with peers where they hear talk of products in the works at competitors' shops. "Professional people in companies tend to exchange information," notes Carl Ball, of George J. Ball Inc. "I hope our people are getting as much as they are giving at trade shows." Engineers at steel minimills in the United States routinely trade knowhow on their products and processes with peers at other mills. Often the information traded is proprietary.

Pulled together in one place, these bits and pieces of information can reveal a striking mosaic of a competitor's strategy. Fuld recommends that small companies appoint one person to take responsibility for "massaging the data

Break the big question into smaller ones for which data can be collected. Then hit the streets.

and getting it around the company." He likens such a person to a ringmaster who directs the audience's attention to what is going on in each ring of the circus. Mixing the metaphor, he also describes the person as a "human switchbox" who makes sure incoming data gets to the decision-makers and back out to those in the field.

While MBAs are useful in analyzing the data, the experienced employee with a long memory, a fat Rolodex, and packed files brings an essential perspective to the process. For years a marketing director at Adolph Coors Co. kept files of news articles and government reports on competitors. One day executives of the family owned beer company came to him with a disturbing report: There were rumors that a competitor was going to push sales in an area dominated by Coors, and might even open a plant there. What should the company do?

By studying his files, the marketing director was able to conclude that the competitor's existing plants were already producing at full capacity and that it would take at least two years for them to build a new plant in the area. Coors decided it didn't need to worry about the competitor in that area for at least two years. The marketing director's files and judgment thus saved the company millions of dollars that it would have spent on promotion and advertising to combat the competitor's strategy.

Though one employee with a well-stocked file and memory can make a difference, a small company may very well want to do better. Another consultant, Jan Herring, argues that corporate intelligence can't be done part time by a single employee. Herring, a former CIA employee who set up Motorola's business intelligence program and is now with the Futures Group in Glastonbury, Connecticut, believes that, at minimum, a company should dedicate "two brains and a library" to the work.

One of the two should have the mind of a collector, absorbing what he hears. The other person should have a more analytical bent, a mind that restlessly searches out and sees patterns in masses of raw data. This tends to be an executive responsible for plans and strategy, who can enlist salesmen in the collection.

Experts in the field cheerfully report that you can find out almost anything about the competition if you know where to look. The rule, says Fuld, is to follow the money. Whenever money is exchanged, information is too. Every deal generates myriad documents, some of which find their way into public files at government agencies and courthouses; others into newspapers, magazines, and trade journals. Information itself spreads geometrically from the principals through consultants, analysts, employees, journalists, and government officials. As any good reporter will tell you, a few calls can plug you into a network that can supply rich details about your competitors.

Most trade shows are "a lot of little feet walking around with big ears," says Leonard Fuld. The companies that do the best job of covering these shows, he says, usually get their people together beforehand, discuss what they would like to learn about competitors at the show, the major questions they'd like to answer. They may assign people to cover specific company booths or to pay particular attention to competitors' marketing or pricing strategies. When they return home, they may meet and discuss what they found out and circulate a transcript to others in the company.

All sorts of regulatory bodies, from the federal Environmental Protection Agency to the state labor department or local zoning board, make companies submit data on compliance that is open to the public. But you have to know the rules for ferreting it out. If you get a denial from a federal agency, try to obtain the information under the federal Freedom of Information Act, which requires agencies to make most information available to the public. Many states have their own version of the law.

Industry studies published by firms such as Frost and Sullivan are expensive but contain a wealth of detail (call and ask to see a table of contents first if you want to make sure the subjects covered pertain to your interests). Investment analysts and stock brokerage firms issue reports on companies that can be helpful; many are summarized in special newspapers or databases.

National publications such as magazines, trade journals, and newsletters do not normally cover local and regional businesses. For this information, many companies have to regularly scan local newspapers and other sources closer to home. A few good sources that are frequently overlooked are:

The library. Some libraries are a treasure trove of information about local companies. Leila Kight of Washington Researchers says that libraries may keep archives and even recent reports on companies. "Often we've gone there and found very proprietary information—memos from top executives to one another, that sort of thing." On the library shelves in one town, Kight's researchers found an exhaustive study of a locally based food company by the Boston Consulting Group that probably cost thousands of dollars and was only six months old.

Local universities. They're often engaged in joint ventures, case studies, or corporate R&D. Class projects, mas-

ters' theses, and doctoral dissertations may be rich source of information, says Kight. Abstracts of academic theses can be found on CD-ROM disc distributed by University Microfilms International, Ann Arbor, Michigan.

Meetings of civic associations. Top executives of local companies often speak at meetings of the Rotary, the Jaycees, or the Chamber of Commerce. They have every reason to want to pat themselves on the back and often talk freely about their business plans and accomplishments.

The tax assessor's office and the firehouse. Both are likely to have plans of a local factory on file, complete with details of the machinery, number of people working there, materials used in processing, and so on. Fire departments keep such plans in case they have to go into the plants during emergencies. They're not obliged to show them to you, but might if you ask nicely.

Newspaper clippings. A variety of national clipping services regularly monitor newspapers and magazines across the country. They'll supply clippings on your competitors in other cities, but if you don't want to spend a lot, try to limit the number of subjects you ask them to cover. There are also many online services you can access yourself.

Help wanted ads. Very often they provide clues to a competitor's strategy, its future plans and new product development. "You hire R&D people, scientists, years in advance," Fuld notes. Also, ads that spell out salaries and benefits and details on shifts reveal a lot about a company's overhead.

State Uniform Commercial Codes. Almost all states have a uniform commercial code, which, when a company borrows money, requires the lender to file data on the purposes of the loan. The file kept in the state capital may contain all sorts of information and can be seen on request.

Reporters and editors. Much of what they know about the businesses they cover never gets into articles. Fuld and other analysts suggest calling sources cited in news stories and even the reporters themselves. If the reporter doesn't have time, he'll probably get you off his back by giving you the best name he can think of. Then you call that person and say so-and-so, the reporter, told you to call. Suddenly you're in the network!

The busy, overburdened owner of a family business may now be pleading for mercy. All right, he may be saying, I can find out lots of things about my competitors that I never bothered to ask. But how can I frame the questions so I'm sure of getting useful answers and my staff and I are not swamped?

The trick is to break the big question into smaller ones for which data can be collected. If you ask a researcher to find out your competitor's marketing strategy, you may draw a blank. But if you explain you want to know what the competitor spends on advertising, what trade shows they go to, where their sales offices are located, how many people are in each office, their pricing on projects up for bid, there are ways of getting answers. For example, the researcher can consult with Leading National Advertisers (LNA) in New York City, which keeps databases on advertising expenditures by company, by product, and by medium.

To get a full picture of a competitor's strategy, data should be collected and interpreted continuously, not just once a year when management takes up the strategic plan. The information should be shared throughout the company, and employees who pass it along should not be shy about offering their own analyses of it. Even in smaller companies, employees may fear censure if they reach conclusions that turn out to be wrong. One manager of a pharmaceutical company complained after reading a detailed 10-page memo from a subordinate in R&D: "I don't know what he's ultimately telling me." Though precise and accurate, the memo lacked any overall assessment.

As Carl Ball found out, employees in smaller companies may be reluctant to spend too much time on intelligence meetings and documentation. They are under pressure to produce profits and please customers and don't see an immediate payoff, so they tend to rely on old habits and channels for their information.

In family companies, the owners impart a powerful impetus to an intelligence program simply by letting staff know they think it's important. Fuld suggests that information sharing on competitors might be an item on the agenda of family retreats that many companies hold once a year with management. But, he adds, the company should also review the latest reports at monthly intervals between retreats. A large and far flung family network can also be helpful in the collection process. He suggests that family members in charge of subsidiaries in other cities keep clippings on local competitors and regularly send them to the main office.

By becoming more alert to intelligence, family businesses can also be astute about sealing off leaks in their own company. The competitors, too, may have sleuths lurking out there ware are ready to pounce on every scrap of information; you should avoid making their job too easy.

Private companies have an edge in that they are not forced to disclose financial data. But some families have squabbles and succession problems that spill over into the business. The dissension reflects weaknesses that can be exploited by competitors. It isn't easy to seal the lips of discontented family members, but the family's leaders must repeatedly emphasize the importance of discretion to survival of the enterprise. They should warn family members who are not in the business but hear inside information at home or at family council meetings not to discuss it with outsiders.

Beyond that, Fuld advises family businesses to take the same precautions as other companies. For example, ask employees to sign a basic secrecy agreement; keep warning them about discussing sensitive information at trade shows; ask them to lock away important papers in a desk drawers before leaving the office at night; for sensitive documents use the new kinds of paper that do not permit copying; stamp such documents "Confidential" in red.

While many family businesses are secretive, some may regard these preventative measures as slightly paranoid. But information counts heavily in today's marketplace, and the easygoing firm can go out of business if it does not pay attention to security.

The most controversial question raised about competitor intelligence may be even harder to answer for family owned firms: where to draw the line on behavior that may be unethical.

Intelligence researchers usually proclaim that everything they do is legal and above board. Leonard Fuld has

Ten commandments for business sleuths

I. Thou shalt not lie when representing thyself. (for example, "I am a poor humble student writing a term paper...").

II. Thou shalt not swap misinformation.

III. Thou shalt not bribe.

IV. Thou shalt not plant eavesdropping devices.

V. Thou shalt not knowingly pump someone for information if it may sacrifice that person's job or reputation.

VI. Thou shalt not deliberately mislead anyone in an interview.

VII. Thou shalt not steal a trade secret (or steal competitors' employees away in hopes of learning a trade secret).

VIII. Thou shalt not secretly tape-record an interview.

IX. Thou shalt not swap price information with thy competitor.

X. Thou shalt observe thy company's legal guidelines as set fourth by thy legal counsel.

written a Ten Commandments of intelligence gathering, a code of good behavior that rules out bribery and deception (opposite). When his staff visits the town hall or firehouse and asks to look at a company's file, for example, they explain exactly who they are and what they are doing without identifying the client and usually leave their card.

As in popular movies involving small-town conspiracies, local officials may immediately get on the phone after the visit and inform plant managers that strangers have been snooping around the place. Sometimes, Fuld then hears from the CEO who wants to make sure the researchers "have gotten accurate information."

While coaxing information from town officials who are not obliged to show it to them is not illegal, it doubtless raises some eyebrows in the community. Likewise, although researchers have a right to stand outside a factory's gates and count the workers coming out of cars in the parking lot (in order to assess the total number employed there), or sit in a local bar and listen to conversations between employees, the natives may well consider this spying.

Family owned businesses thrive on their reputation in the community, their personal values and honesty in dealing with customers. For them, active snooping may be obnoxious or at least awkward; and it may be harmful. While local businesses are often aggressive seekers of information on competitors, and everybody does it, they must be careful not to go too far and violate local norms.

When weighing any given method of intelligence gathering, Fuld says, the ultimate acid test may be in the stomach. In other words, if your stomach acids are churning, it's probably wrong or, at least, you think it is.

Fuld also talks about "the active-passive line." He illustrates the distinction in his seminars by describing a real case. While waiting to see someone at a printing plant, a marketing manager for McNeilab, makers of Tylenol, noticed a new ad for Datril, a competing product, tacked to the board. The marketing manager couldn't help reading the ad, which contained details of a new promotion campaign and pricing strategy for Datril. Upon leaving the plant, he sped back to his office and informed management of the details.

Nobody in the seminar usually faults him for doing that, Fuld says; the printer was basically to blame for leaving sensitive information where visitors could see it. The marketing manager was *passive* in the sense that he could hardly avoid reading it.

But Fuld then leads his seminar participants into a deeper ethical quagmire. "I change the case around and ask: What if there is a tarpaulin covering that ad and the waiting executive can only make out one corner of it with the words 'Top Secret—New Pricing Plans for Datril.' It's a stormy day, and the receptionist announces, 'I'm leaving early to beat the storm,' and the McNeilab guy is left there, by his lonesome, waiting for his appointment. Does he lift the tarp?

"A minority will say, 'Sure.'" Fuld goes on. "Others will say, 'If I slide over to the stand and accidentally knock it over, and if the board lands right side up, I'm a lucky man.' Most of those in the room say that they would not touch the tarpaulin. But I'm sure if I took each of them into a confessional booth and asked him separately, I'd get different answers."

—*Howard Muson*

Reengineering

When to reorganize, and how to do it right

Corporate change is best undertaken before trouble begins, not after. Here's how to transform company processes, revitalize management, improve efficiency—and build support for what will be a tumultuous transformation.

HALLMARK CARDS was doing just fine in 1989 when the head of its core business looked over the horizon and saw trouble. The once-homogeneous greeting card market had fragmented into numerous markets serving a bewildering variety of niche customer segments. Unless it could rationalize its production to respond more rapidly to changing customer tastes, Hallmark—still controlled by the Hall family and the dominant company in the greeting card industry—might see its markets picked off one by one by smaller competitors.

This looming competitive threat convinced Robert L. Stark, president of Hallmark's Personal Communications Group (PCG), to launch a program to totally re-engineer Hallmark processes. What was unusual about Hallmark's campaign, as described in the best-selling *Reengineering the Corporation* by Michael Hammer and James Champy, was that it was "not a response to any life-threatening problem but a farsighted effort to keep such problems out of the company's future." For Hallmark, reengineering was a preemptive competitive strike.

Underperforming and financially distressed businesses usually become that way because they were unable or unwilling to change processes or to adapt to new and changing markets and customer demands. Change, however, is best undertaken in anticipation of trouble, while a company is still relatively healthy—as in the Hallmark case—rather than after a crisis occurs.

The kind of transformation that may result from reengineering is sometimes scary for managers and employees and not easy to accomplish. Hammer and Champy themselves estimate that 50 to 70 percent of companies that undertake it fail for various reasons, most of which spring from a lack of understanding of what reengineering involves and of the organizational commitment required to make the radical innovations that are often necessary.

Change—even carefully planned change—involves risks, and some family business owners are not willing to take big risks unless there is a question of business survival. Ironically, family firms that were founded on principles of innovation and entrepreneurship often reach a stage when security is more important to the owners than building wealth. They are not willing to contemplate major organizational changes.

Yet family firms, by their very nature, may be better able to succeed at process reengineering than most nonfamily companies. Because of the concentration of ownership in these businesses, their leaders, once committed to the idea, are able to move decisively to do the thorough assessment of the company's processes and implement the long-term changes that are needed. When business survival is threatened, the desire to preserve the business for future generations and to maintain the family's status in the community become powerful motivators. The fact that many owners have given personal guarantees to lenders and suppliers, which puts their own wealth on the line, is another strong incentive to ensure the long-term profitability of the enterprise. Moreover, younger leaders of the company, who have not yet built their wealth, may be more willing than their seniors to take drastic steps to ensure the long-range viability of the company.

What exactly is reengineering, and what is it not? To begin with, it has little to do with the old-fashioned industrial engineering that is familiar to companies that have been around for some time. In the old days, industrial engineers came into plants, closely scrutinized how people worked, and recommended ways in which bottlenecks could be eliminated and the work organized more efficiently. These kinds of efficiency studies can lead to improvements. However, their greatest value lies in the enthusiasm that they generate in management for more extensive changes that will benefit the bottom line dramatically.

Modern-day reengineering is based on the perception that in some companies mere tinkering will not be sufficient to maintain their competitiveness. It examines a company's processes—production, the handling of orders, inventory management—in the context of organizational structure, costs, and overall market considerations. Often these functions are managed by separate departments with lines of responsibility from the top to the bottom of the organization and with very little communication between them.

The extensive analysis that is the first step in reengineering may trigger changes not only in specific processes but in organizational structure, job design, and management systems. The perception in the ranks of many companies that "reengineering" is simply a code word for massive job cuts is mistaken. Although work force reductions are occasionally a byproduct of reengineering, they are made only after a sophisticated analysis of comparative costs. Too many companies lay off workers first and ask questions later.

Above all, reengineering should be totally focused on serving the customer, on determining the best way to deliver the goods and services that the customer wants, when he or she wants them. Usually, the best way becomes obvious when the company reexamines its processes in the context of how it goes to market. When business owners say, "I am willing to change our processes totally if that is what it takes to serve our customers better," they are ready for business process reengineering. The structural changes undertaken at Hallmark were all organized around point-of-sale computerized systems installed at Hallmark-owned stores to record sales for different lines of greeting cards. With this new system, production of cards and deliveries to retailers were more closely tailored to shifts in customer demand. The system was the key to a team approach to management that quickened the development and delivery of new products.

Many owners make the mistake of relying on their sales force to keep them informed about what customers want and how the company's performance is perceived. But the customers know a lot more about the company's operation and its ability to deliver than the sales people ever find out. The customers usually do their homework on suppliers. They know not just that their deliveries are sometimes late or that the supplier's product is not always consistent in quality. They usually have insights into whether the company is functionally organized, what management weaknesses it has, what problems it has in its markets, whether it has bottlenecks in production scheduling, and what kinds of inventory management problems it faces.

Business owners who are not in touch with these perceptions may wake up one day and find that their customers have drifted away. The experience of a family owned textile manufacturer with $35 million in sales was typical. The company, a producer of high-volume, low-margin commodity yarns, was losing business to competitors. The family managers felt compelled to compete on price, even though the business had been built on its reputation for product quality and service. With lower prices, the company's gross margins fell. The family's habitual response to low margins was to increase volume. Family managers were happiest when the plant was humming at full capacity. So they began to produce more, and more, and more.

To increase production, however, the company had to buy new machinery. The increased internal costs eventually wiped out the company's slim profit margins. The more the company produced, the more money it was losing. Cash became tight and suppliers and lenders brought pressure on the company for payment, further accelerating the decline. Competitors, meanwhile, seemed to be thriving while operating on normal production schedules.

The family clung to the status quo until it become fully clear that without dramatic changes, the company might disappear. The first step was to consult the company's customers. When the family leaders did that, they discovered that customers felt they could get commodity yarns from many suppliers and that what they really needed was high-quality colored cotton, for which they were willing to pay a premium.

After much soul-searching, the family decided to change its strategy to produce these specialty yarns. It revamped its production facility, introducing customized systems to react swiftly to smaller-volume orders for different colors of cotton. The specialty yarns were not only produced by shorter runs, but required greater attention to scheduling, setup, timely delivery, and quality. Now that the company was going to market with a new product, the sales force had to be reorganized and staffed differently. The sales people had to focus on solving customer problems and not just selling high volume.

The change in strategy not only increased gross margins but served as a catalyst for a dramatic cost-cutting

> *Someone must champion the cause. Tell top managers their jobs are on the line.*

program under which management was reorganized, staff was reduced, and an underutilized plant was idled. After two years in which the company was losing $2 million annually, it began to operate at break-even and has survived as a going concern.

This family clung to the status quo until it was almost too late. Although it has succeeded in reversing the company's decline, management could have moved much sooner to address the company's problems. In a turnaround situation, the company must first be stabilized and its balance sheet fixed. To contemplate changes in such turbulent circumstances is both disruptive and scary—although at this point reengineering may be the only remedy.

Family business owners often resist considering such remedies for a number of reasons. For one thing, they tend to be closer to their employees than leaders of large publicly owned corporations and reluctant to take any action that might require a work force reduction or management reorganization. For another, the fact that the leaders wear two hats—they are both owners and managers—tends to paralyze their will when embarrassing decisions must be made. The effective manager might see the need to overhaul operations and lay off people in order to save the company and the rest of its loyal employees. But owners often have an image of themselves—many are put on a pedestal in the community—that prevents them from taking steps that would amount to an admission of failure and a loss of face. Thus, the leader of the textile manufacturing firm dreaded the prospect of idling the underutilized plant, even though, as a good manager, he saw the need for it quite plainly. In other cases, the senior generation is simply satisfied with what it has accomplished and is no longer driven to build more wealth.

Clearly, in order to undertake process reengineering, companies must be powerfully motivated to change. If the program is not driven by the instinct for survival, it must be stimulated by something else. When top management approaches the program on little cat feet, when it refuses to examine real problems for fear of disrupting the operation or unsettling employees, it greatly diminishes the prospects for success. Yet we've found that the owner who is willing to acknowledge problems and admit mistakes earns the respect of employees—and can often mobilize their support for change.

Members of the second generation can play a key role, perhaps because they have a large stake in the long-term survival of the company and in building their own net worth. While an owner may see little risk to his already funded retirement plan from maintaining the status quo, a daughter may view reengineering as the only way to meet her expectations for a future livelihood and to increase the value of her estate.

Many companies fail at reengineering because of a lack of follow-through on the analysis of their processes. Companies spend huge sums on studies, then fail to implement the changes that are necessary, usually because of the same resistance that prevented the company from addressing the problems in the first place—bureaucratic inertia, fear of radical change, old habits of thinking. Three major elements are essential to effective follow-through: 1) the continued presence of outside "change agents," 2) a business plan that sets out specific goals, assigns tasks, and establishes a timetable for their completion, and 3) a management reorganization to ensure effective monitoring and implementation of the plan.

The outside expert's role in the early stages of the engagement is to analyze the factors that have led to the company's decline and, in turnaround situations, ensure that enough cash is generated to stabilize the firm. The outsider then has a continued role to play in professionalizing management and making certain the staff is equipped to direct the new operations. Unless new, interim management is brought in, the existing management must be trained to operate in a vastly different, reengineered environment.

The business plan provides financial projections and a narrative of the future with numbers attached to it. For example, it may provide that a certain plant will be shut down by November 30; or the company's head count will be reduced from 150 to 100 by that date, while the sales force is increased from 15 to 20. Unlike budgets, formal plans include written assumptions that allow management to both monitor and implement the required steps. At the same time, it allows other stakeholders such as inactive family shareholders and lenders to monitor the company's progress.

A final key factor for success in reengineering is the presence of a champion. One of the problems of reengineering in large public companies is that division managers sometimes see the process as just another in a series of top management fads which will eventually be forgotten. They don't sense that top management has an enduring commitment to it unless the chairman declares, "Division presidents, I am serious about seeing that this plan is carried out. Your jobs are on the line."

Reassure employees that change is necessary and positive—in meetings, newsletters, videos.

Although some owners of family businesses see their employees as extended family, they nevertheless have difficulty communicating the message that change is necessary. Because a family owner has singular power and stature, however, he or she is in a far better position to get the company moving than the leader of a public company who must answer to many more stakeholders.

When Hallmark employees began to worry that the company's traditional values and beliefs would be threatened by the vast reengineering changes in the company, they were reassured by Donald J. Hall, the company's chairman and the son of the founder. As Robert Stark, head of the Personal Communications Group, recalled: "Don wrote five beliefs and four guiding values that were communicated to all 22,000 Hallmark employees over several months through private and group meetings; articles in the company's internal magazine; and videos featuring Hall, CEO Irvine Hockaday Jr., and other senior executives. Once we had effectively communicated this message, everyone understood that while we would change our ability to get to market, we wouldn't change our beliefs and values. That for us was a critical first step to create a change process focused on results."

The chairman of a smaller family company—a manufacturer of lanterns with several plants—personally visited each of his plants with members of our team and announced at each site, "People, this is something we are going to do." His presence left a powerful impression and no doubt contributed to the successful implementation of the reengineering process.

The owner of a retail hardware chain with $10 million in sales confessed his own concerns to employees while explaining the difficulties of reengineering the company's inventory and merchandising strategies. "I feel like I'm standing on a rock in the middle of a rushing stream," he said. "If I stay here or go back, I'm going to get wet and, in fact, I may drown. Well, darn it, if I'm going to get wet, I might as well do it going forward. I will get to the other side." The employees appreciated his candor, and wholeheartedly supported the reengineering plan. There was a true champion.

— Baker A. Smith

— V —

ADVISORS AND CONSULTANTS

◆

SOONER OR LATER you will need one: an outside advisor or consultant. Although owners are naturally reluctant to admit they need help, the smart ones who do seek outsiders find they benefit enormously, both from the fresh perspective and technical skills outsiders can provide. The question is not whether to hire outsiders, but when to hire them, how to find the best ones for your company, and how to best utilize them.

A board of directors is the ultimate source of advice, and the hardest group of outsiders to form and manage. Chapter 21 explains when to start a board, how to choose board members and set their course, and how to make the most effective, ongoing use of a board.

Chapter 22 addresses individual advisors: family business consultants, lawyers, and insurance agents. It tells how to select the right people and sustain a productive relationship. Well chosen and managed, each advisor can provide a critical capability that can help the business grow and the family profit.

Boards of Directors

Why you should have a board

Virtually all family business consultants, researchers—and owners themselves—agree that an advisory board or board of directors is vital to long term success. Why?

MOST FAMILY COMPANIES are owner operated and the only board of directors they have is a fictitious entity, written about in contrived documents, that is designed to protect the corporate shell in the eyes of the IRS. Most owner-managers don't want to bear the cost of a real board. They don't want to spend their time educating outside board members in the family business. They want to be free to make decisions, when they want to make them, without interference from a board.

But conditions change. The owner-manager gets tired of shouldering total responsibility. It comes time to let others take over day-to-day management. Changes are called for, but there is no one there to manage the process. Founders don't have a clue how to manage their own letting go. Successors aren't sure how to step up to the plate and frequently lack the skills and support to do so effectively. Circumstances compel the creation of a board to ensure a smooth transition, but the idea encounters deep resistance.

Boards of closely held companies serve mostly in an advisory capacity to the principal owners. They usually have little real authority and seldom vote on major issues. The directors serve to clarify the goals of the company, to articulate plans, to enhance communication among the owners, to build consensus for initiatives that might otherwise be contentious and divisive.

The challenge for boards of family companies is not only to provide good corporate governance that is responsive to the needs of the company, but to recognize and deal with the pragmatic realities and idiosyncrasies of the family owners.

Over time the mission of the board changes, and so should its composition. In the early years, for example, family members may be appointed to the board in order to prepare them for future managerial or ownership responsibilities. Later, as the family engages in succession planning, the board may have to confront a recalcitrant founder. When a process for resolving family conflicts and succession issues has been put in place, much greater emphasis in board appointments can then be given to business and technical expertise.

Outside directors are always helpful, but the type and number of such directors should depend on the board's mission. If the issue is a recalcitrant founder, for example, the chief executive of a major corporation is not likely to be the best choice. CEOs who take professionalism for granted may not have the patience to deal with the founder's irrational behavior. In contrast, advisors to the founder, who have earned his trust and confidence are much more likely to be effective in this situation. True "strangers" rarely work well as directors in the emergence phase of family business boards.

Only in mature family companies do boards begin to operate like the boards of public companies. In later generations, the number of inactive shareholders begins to grow. There may also be different branches of the family wanting representation on the board. Increasingly, outside board members are called on to mediate conflicts between active and inactive family members, and between families. The board must set and monitor standards of professionalism and ensure that the corporation is being run in the best interests of the shareholders. A strong outside influence is needed to establish impartiality.

In designing the board, structure follows strategy: Look at the company's business goals and design accordingly. With a sound design and a shrewd mix of members, a board can reduce insularity, increase adaptability, and provide stability in times of rapid change. More and more, the family business can't survive without one.

— *Peter Davis*

When to start a board of directors

If your company is young or small you may not be ready for a board, or need one. In the meantime, however, an advisory board can provide help.

MOST FAMILY BUSINESSES require significant evolution before they can benefit from a board of directors. Often, a board does not become highly effective until the company is through the "threshold" transition between entrepreneurial venture and professional management. To respond to business and family needs during the transition, an advisory board, or advisory council, may be more useful.

Family businesses usually go through a difficult period when they have grown beyond the founder's direct influence but have not yet professionalized management. Some companies take longer—perhaps generations—to cross the threshold, and size appears to have little to do with how quickly the transition occurs. Even large organizations can function for some time in this twilight zone.

The essential milestones that a company must pass in evolving toward professionalism are:

1. Adequate, formalized shareholder agreements.

2. Agreement on goals and objectives for the business as an investment (growth objectives, tolerable risk levels, returns expected, and so on).

3. Timely, accurate accounting information, in a form that facilitates planning, operational decision-making, and performance review (for example, operating and capital budgets, and regular key-results reports).

4. Strong, coordinated middle management, motivated by an incentive compensation plan that is geared to achieving performance goals.

Most business founders require some professional or technical advice from the beginning, if only to draw up partnership agreements and satisfy tax reporting requirements. The need for this kind of expertise continues to grow as the business evolves.

For the most part, however, the typical entrepreneur has tunnel vision when starting out; he relies on drive, adrenaline, and persistence to punch through barriers and reach goals. True outside review, by contrast, is inherently analytical, critical, questioning—in clear conflict with the entrepreneur's style.

In a perfect world, such conflict in style could be intellectually stimulating. In the real world, however, survival is a white-knuckle thing, like barnstorming. The entrepreneur feels he can study the fine points of flying later. What he needs now is not back-seat instructors. Just give him a good mechanic or two.

Eventually, however, the business owner's afterburners begin to sputter, and he looks around for suggestions on how he can power up for the next phase of growth. He needs a brain to pick, a sounding board.

At this stage, he or she usually looks for advice from professional advisors, consultants, or peers in the industry. In most cases, these people have in-depth knowledge of the workings of the business and the specific characteristics of the owner's industry. That is not what one normally looks for in outside directors, who are supposed to be knowledgeable about business in general. Outside directors are there to provide an objective view of the company, not to confirm the owner's assumptions and biases. Instead, through the threshold phase, most owner-managers can get more benefit from technical professionals or industry peers. (In some industries, groups of CEOs who get to know each other form review groups that periodically descend upon a member to evaluate his or her business.)

Still, important issues arise during the transition period that require specific expertise rather than objective review. For example, the company usually needs help in bringing the shareholders together in agreement on goals and objectives. The family also needs intensive help in planning the management succession. They face questions about successor competence; the rights and benefits of family managers; selection of future key managers; and a sensible, secure retirement plan for the present owner. Outside directors rarely have the time or expertise for such hands-on work.

Along with a succession plan, the family needs to achieve agreement on the transfer of ownership. This is not merely a question of estate planning. There are also questions to be answered about the ownership structure that will be put in place, of who will have voting power and control, of what capitalization strategies and buy-sell agreements are appropriate.

These issues can seldom be decided without guidance from professionals in law, accounting, insurance, and family business management. Few outside directors have the necessary training, experience, or inclination to offer advice on these matters. And until the basic questions are resolved, few businesses or families can address strategic issues—the outside director's meat and potatoes—effectively.

Gradually, the need for such professional advice declines in the threshold period as the management team takes shape. Ownership issues have been settled; operating issues are increasingly analyzed and tested internally, and the next- generation leaders begin to take charge.

Only then, as management develops a strategic focus, does the business begin to have a significant need for the kind of independent, long-range thinking that an outside board of directors can provide. Up to that point, however, an advisory board can do a much better job laying track. The advisory board may consist of an accountant, an attorney, the senior owner-managers, perhaps an industry consultant, and possibly a representative of non-participating shareholders.

Few experts would argue that non-participating shareholders are appropriate for outside boards. But through the threshold phase, the support of these shareholders is often essential. Their membership on an advisory board is natural and acceptable; it also offers an opportunity to educate them and gain their support.

Perhaps the greatest worth of an advisory board during the threshold phase is to ensure continuity and coordination. Too often in family business transitions, experts are allowed to give advice in compartments and the process moves by fits and starts, because there is no formal organization to oversee it. By setting up an advisory board that meets regularly, with agendas and minutes, the owners ensure continuity in attention to the issues, coordinated action, and implementation of decisions. The owners also become comfortable with the notion of review by outsiders, which paves the way for the long-run ideal of a true board of directors.

— *Donald J. Jonovic*

Choosing the right board members… and setting a course

Forget consultants and friends. Look for hands-on industry people not tied to your company. Then give them a unifying goal.

OUTSIDE DIRECTORS are one of the richest and least-used resources available to private companies today. By most estimates, only a small fraction of private firms in the United States have boards with outsiders on them. More often, boards are composed of shareholders, family members, and figureheads who meet to rubber-stamp resolutions. In some firms, lawyers write fictional minutes of meetings that never took place.

Business owners' fears about active outside boards usually turn out to be unfounded. Most owners who do convene a board of directors find that it helps them tackle major issues without robbing them of control, independence, or any meaningful measure of privacy.

An active board can benefit almost any firm with 50 or more employees. For professional service firms, the threshold is even lower, at about 20 employees. (Smaller firms can benefit from forming an informal two- or three-member advisory council that includes respected peers or the corporate lawyer, accountant, or consultant, as noted in the previous item.)

Ideally, the board should be in place before the company reaches major—and sometimes predictable—corporate metamorphoses. Often, for instance, a company hits an "entrepreneurial plateau" at about 40 to 80 employees, where the business outstrips the entrepreneur's ability to run it alone and, as a result, stagnates or loses its strategic focus. At this point, the owner often experiences burnout and badly needs energy from an active board.

A board can also be particularly helpful during a change in corporate leadership. The continual guidance of trusted, experienced outside directors can provide a kind of insurance policy, guaranteeing that the transition will be smooth and orderly. A broadening of ownership, a change in industry structure, or the onset of new forms of competition, technology, or regulation can pose similar challenges, taxing even the most vital and skilled manager.

Composition of board members. The board should be kept relatively small, with usually no more than seven members. The ideal board consists of only outside directors, plus the CEO as chairman. One or two insiders may supplant the outsiders, but only if they are substantial equity partners.

Of course, anyone who is a major stockholder, or who represents a branch of a family with major stockholdings, has a right to a seat on the board. These partners in the business cannot be excluded. If ownership is dispersed among several branches of a family represented by four different directors, then outside directorships will probably have to be limited to three or four, to keep the board a manageable size.

If branches of the family each have substantial shareholdings, voting trusts can be established, with designated trustees representing each branch on the board. This can help unify shareholders and avoid politicking and maverick activity by dissatisfied or restless individuals with small holdings.

Especially in the first round of director selections, the CEO should make sure that all key shareholders are comfortable with the nominees. The veto concept should apply here: If a shareholder or family member is not confident from the beginning that a candidate will be a good, trustworthy director, then the CEO should reject that candidate without grilling the shareholder or family member on his or her reasons.

At the same time, the CEO should guard against letting the selection process deteriorate into a contest among various constituencies. This can yield a constituency board, with each director feeling a sense of responsibility to a particular shareholder group. This setup can cause major problems in the event of a shareholder dispute.

To see that everything goes smoothly, the business owner can sometimes designate a trusted associate or outsider—a consultant, a director, an accountant, attorney, or banker—to act as an objective facilitator for the board selection process.

Who should not be asked to serve. "Whom do I leave off?" is the first question many owners ask when establishing an active outside board. "How can I possibly include on my board all the deserving candidates—my customers, my suppliers, my old friends, my banker, my accountant, . my lawyer, my family, my vice president of sales…?"

The answer: Leave them all off.

Politics, bolstering egos, repaying debts, conveying thanks, rewarding performance, satisfying interest groups—ideally, none of these factors should play a role in selecting directors. Instead, the CEO should design the board with one purpose in mind: to meet the needs of the company as well as the needs of the CEO as the leader of the business. Let us look at the strengths and weaknesses of various kinds of outside board candidates:

Top-management directors. The widespread practice of reaching into top-management ranks for directors has significant drawbacks for the CEO intent on making the most of the board. The presence of senior managers can inhibit board discussion of such confidential matters as succession, management compensation, organizational development, and so on. It also can reduce opportunities for the business owner to be truly candid—to doff his or her "employer" hat and discuss deep-seated doubts, fears, and questions.

This does not mean that the insiders should be excluded from board meetings. The controller or other top executives may be included in most, or even all board sessions. But management insiders should always be present by invitation; that preserves the CEO's right to ask them to excuse themselves when sensitive issues arise.

Competitors. Competitors or potential competitors should never be directors, for obvious reasons. Directors serving on competitors' boards should be ruled out, too; the law prohibits "interlocking directorates," wherein the same people serve on the boards of competing companies.

Consultants. The services of these professionals are already available to the business owner, and they bring to the boardroom an inherent conflict of interest. These people work for you. They're not the right people to challenge you.

Some business owners find that it pays to make exceptions for advisors who have broad exposure to top executives of a wide range of businesses. These professionals often develop executive skills and can be a valuable resource, even if they lack experience in starting or running a company. Paid advisors should not dominate the board, though.

Trust, patience, and values are vital qualities

In choosing directors, a family might look for individuals with strong general management experience, or it might seek a variety of experts who can provide advice in areas of the business that have become vital to the company's future success, such as core technologies, research and development, marketing, and finance. But there are overriding criteria in the selection of directors that can make or break the board.

Principal among them is the chemistry between the founder and the candidate. Does the candidate have the founder's trust? Does he or she have credibility in the founder's eyes? When the founder is resistant to change, board members are going to spend most of their time challenging "the old man." Do they have the motivation and skill to challenge effectively? Is there enough trust in the relationship for the founder to bear this constructive challenge?

To challenge effectively, board members have to know when to push and when to back off; they must be skilled at depersonalizing discussion of sensitive issues. When the owner-manager refuses to listen—so often the case—the members must doggedly persist and have enormous reserves of patience.

The board also plays an important role in empowering a successor. Board members should be good teachers and have the time and patience for mentoring. The board's role in succession is to support the younger generation in building their vision of the company's future and helping them put together plans to implement that vision.

In the end, the best directors have those important qualities that rarely show up on conventional lists: Good listener, good mentor, patience, and values compatible with family goals and culture.
— *Peter Davis*

Friends. Friends are harder to find than directors, and their counsel is usually freely available anyway. Why jeopardize a good friendship by subjecting it to the stresses of the boardroom?

Retirees. While retirees can be excellent directors, the CEO should be cautious about overusing them. One reason is that retirees sometimes lose touch with the mainstream of business. Another is that directorships can become too important to them. If holding seats on corporate boards is a major source of stimulation and ego support, the retiree can become so fearful of losing the directorships that his judgment is compromised.

Academics. In some cases, people from universities, schools, charities, think tanks, or other organizations can be excellent directors. Arguably, they also tend to be more available than corporate CEOs. Nevertheless, the performance-driven business owner takes a risk when he enlists someone without experience in running a profit-making organization.

People who hold other directorships. Candidates who already serve on several boards are also risky recruits. First, the business owner may have to offer high fees in order to compete for their services. Second, the appeal of the learning opportunities afforded by board membership dims for the person who already serves on several.

Other CEOs, entrepreneurs, and business owners. Risk-taking peers often make the best directors. People from larger private companies who have weathered the crises or surmounted the hurdles that still lie ahead for your company are the best candidates of all. They offer the business owner unparalleled experience, perspective, and empathy.

Division heads. Heads of divisions or subsidiaries of

Items for boards to work on

A board protects the interests of shareholders by insuring that the business is managed responsibly. The board reviews all critical governance issues, including:

• Annual capital and operating budgets.
• Quarterly results against targets.
• Financial policy.
• Management control systems.
• The development and implementation of the company's strategic plan.
• Long term contractual agreements.
• The performance of senior managers.
• Major organizational restructurings.
• Succession plans.
• Employees/community relations.

— *Ivan Lansberg*

big public companies can be good directors. But, as a rule, the business owner should avoid functional vice-presidents, such as heads of marketing or research. If marketing expertise is what you need, for example, find the CEO of a marketing-driven company.

Establishing a mission. Preparing a board prospectus is the first step in organizing an effective board. This one-page to three-page document can be a helpful tool in recruiting director candidates, and it can assist the business owner in networking with lenders, advisors, and others who might know attractive director prospects.

The introductory section of the prospectus usually gives a concise overview of the company, including its size in terms of sales and employees, its relative strengths and weaknesses, and its major strategic goals or challenges. This section should convey a sense of the company's industry, competition, customers, and market. And while the prospectus need not reveal a great deal of financial information, it should offer director candidates a clear sense of the business context.

The second component of the prospectus—the board profile—describes the criteria for board members in terms of experience, skill, and understanding. To reach that point, most CEOs find it useful to ask several preliminary questions.

What is your industry profile? The first step is to thoroughly examine the driving forces in your industry. Is competition fragmented, oligopolistic, or undergoing fundamental change? Are principal markets new, maturing, or expanding internationally? What is the nature of your customers and their buying decisions?

How powerful a role do suppliers play in your industry? What are important characteristics of the regulatory environment? Of your competitors? And what is the state of technology in the industry?

What is your strategic profile? This step requires a look at the company's current stance and direction in relation to its industry. What is its market-share position? Where is its competitive advantage—in differentiating its product or service from others, or in operating at a lower cost? You should consider the labor and capital demands of the business, as well as the role of marketing, R & D, and customer service.

What are the keys to success? Based on the company's current position in a changing industry, what types of tasks, decisions, people, and systems are needed to ensure its success? Does prosperity depend on securing more shelf space from powerful distributors? Does the business require a more highly motivated, fully utilized sales force? Is raising private capital to expand the company's retail

Setting term limits

Experts recommend staggering the terms of board members one, two, or three years. Offer a three-year term to a real catch; a one-year term to a director you might not know so well. With staggered terms, you can maintain continuity by replacing only one or two directors each year. Replacement does not have to be mandatory. You can simply award a good board member with a subsequent term. Some companies require outside directors to rotate off for at least one year after their term expires, to insure the infusion of fresh blood and to easily remove an unsatisfactory director. A limited term may be attractive, and rotation off the board is less awkward than resigning. And remember: If staggered terms and rotation don't work for your company, you can always change your by-laws. — *Gerald Le Van*

branch outlets crucial?

What will be the main sources of future growth? Here, the CEO identifies the most promising new markets or new products, as well as the most important threats to success, including competitive and environmental issues. An analysis of the resources that will likely be needed to secure the future is needed to build a useful board profile.

How will the company's ownership profile affect its future direction? Many business owners seek directors with some understanding of the special ownership and management issues faced by the private business. To that end, it can be helpful to build an ownership profile, describing the relationships among owners, future ownership plans, and so on. A nearly universal question is: How important to us is maintaining private ownership? Another common issue is: How should we address the needs of the growing number of family members who are not working in the business? Basic to this step is an examination of how ownership of the company is likely to evolve in the years to come. Many business owners also include a description of their management style and culture.

Once the business owner has answered these questions, it becomes easier to identify other businesses that demand analogous skills of their executives, and to reach across industry lines to identify candidates who have already reached the goals that are still only objectives for your business.

Aim high. The business owner will want to identify some personal criteria for directors. A few obvious ones should be at the top of the list. Such simple criteria as integrity and courage of conviction can be crucial to a board's success. A desire to learn is an especially appealing trait in directors, and so is a strong team player instinct. Confidentiality, discretion, and tact also show up often on this list.

Another dimension that may be important is entrepreneurial initiative. A person who has spent his whole career at a place like Ford Motor Co. usually has no sense of what it means to be running a $3 million firm.

Some CEOs might wait to find people who have shown that they can sustain a successful family business, or people who have thrived in business partnerships. Others might look for directors who are active in political, civic, and social affairs or who have accumulated significant personal wealth. Experience with wealth can yield valuable lessons, as well as comfort, to the business owner seeking candidates with a similar outlook.

Still others may seek a broad age distribution among directors, perhaps to provide young successors with highly successful peers and role models. Others may strive for a balance between people who are primarily rational and analytical and those who are strongly creative and intuitive. CEOs who have never experienced an effective board might also want to look for people who have served as directors of other successful companies.

In a board search, the business owner should set high standards, seeking out the very best people he or she can find. Candor and thoroughness in the selection process can greatly improve the chances of success. A cross-check of candidates' qualifications with mutual acquaintances is a must. But in the end the business owner has to trust instinct, look for good chemistry, and give top priority to his or her own needs and the requirements of the business. — *John L. Ward*

How to get the most from your board

Start with a clear mission and mandate. Give the board room to maneuver. Review each director's performance. And beware the traps boards can fall or be dragged into.

AT TIMES THERE IS a great deal of unhappiness with the boards of family firms—which means that a very valuable resource is being mismanaged.

Making sure a board succeeds requires hard work on everybody's part. Board members need a mission and a mandate. They need clearly defined boundaries to set off their responsibilities from those of the shareholders and management. They need managers and a CEO who realize that by sharing power, they gain power. In turn, outside directors have to appreciate that family companies are different—and sometimes impose special demands on board members.

If properly managed, a board can be a vital source of insight and support, providing an unemotional forum in which issues too hot for the family to handle alone can be thrashed out.

Many CEOs of family companies are tired of the loneliness of flying solo. Many are sick of being picked on by their families, and see the board as an island of sanity in a sea of troubles. By creating a board with outside directors, moreover, a family CEO will significantly increase his power over the nonbusiness-oriented family shareholders.

The best decisions to share, of course, are the unpopular ones, especially the no-win ones like succession planning. The CEO who has children in the business may be unable to face the emotional consequences of choosing among them. Not only can the board help him make a more objective choice, but by taking some of the responsibility for it, the board can make it more palatable to those who lose out and others affected by the choice.

Boards are also established when power has shifted in significant measure to shareholders, who need a body to present their interests to management. In family businesses, this situation can prove to be more than a little sticky.

Boards of public companies have a hard enough time determining the criteria for judging company decisions. Should they be maximizing shareholder value, whatever that takes? Or do they have a broader responsibility to other "stakeholders"—employees, suppliers, customers, and the public?

In practice, boards have considerable latitude to set their own policy and goals. But what happens in a family business when there are only three or four shareholders and their opinions on the company's direction differ widely?

That is when board members frequently get drawn into efforts to mediate shareholder differences, putting themselves squarely in the middle of a family conflict. To avoid that position—invariably a nightmare—some boards may decide to ignore the shareholders and attempt to make decisions purely on the basis of "what is good for the business." That course, however, is sure to incite stockholding members of the family because it appears that the board is taking the side of management.

Outsiders appointed to the boards of family companies should be free to carry out their valuable role as a highly principled body providing insight and discipline for top management. But they must also know something about the values the family deems important in operating the business. It is the family's job to forge a consensus on values without involving the board, and then to give members of the board a clear mandate which, in turn, enables them to work together with the family as a team. In the long run, a board cannot function without a family consensus, and perhaps the company can't either.

— *Peter Davis*

Choosing consultants

Common fantasies about the consultant's role

A consultant will not succeed unless both he and the client have realistic—and congruent—goals. Avoid hidden assumptions that can lead the process astray.

THERE ARE PROBABLY almost as many reasons for hiring consultants as there are family business owners in America. The most commonly stated ones include: the development of a succession or strategic plan; the design of governance structures such as a board or family council; the management of conflict among family members and between different stakeholders; and, simply, the training of relatives for their various roles. However, certain recurring—and usually hidden—assumptions about the consultant's role among clients seem to complicate matters.

The first casts the consultant in the role of *savior*. He or she can do no wrong and is put on a pedestal by family members as the one who will "fix" all that's wrong with the system. Such inflated expectations carry serious risks. Often influenced by an unconscious wish to "fix" something in their own family background, consultants can easily lose perspective on how much they can actually change in a family business.

The consultant can serve only as a midwife to change; like it or not, the client must deliver the baby. To believe otherwise is a setup for disappointment. Nothing will really change, in fact, until the client takes personal responsibility for seeing that it does.

A second common role that clients hope a consultant will play is that of *reassuring friend*. What clients really want in these cases is not independent judgment but generous amounts of reassurance that "everything is all right." For example, they seek validation that they have been good parents; that their children are, in fact, competent to take over the business; that it will all work out in the end.

The consultant who dislikes confrontation can be easily trapped by the client's denial. He or she may assume a passive role and just coast through the process. After all, no one likes to deliver messages to a parent like: "Sorry, your kid simply does not have what it takes to lead this business." Sooner or later, however, reality catches up with the owner who does not want to face the truth: The successor fails, the business goes into a tailspin, the most competent nonfamily manager quits in frustration. The "reassuring friend" has not been a friend at all but has, in fact, colluded in the development of the crisis.

Third, there are those who hire a consultant to be the *keeper of their secrets*. Typically in these families there is considerable conflict but none of the members dares to raise the issues openly for fear of a meltdown. The consultant is given the impossible mission of trying to bring about change while avoiding all of the issues that the family has refused to face for years.

Fourth, there are those who hire consultants to be their *ambassadors* to the rest of the family, or *allies* against them. These are people who want an outside authority to argue their case for them, to legitimize their opinions with other family members, or even to take up arms against those who hold contrary views. As in the case of those who seek reassurance, these clients may disapprove when the consultant tells them in an initial interview: "Even though you're paying the bill, I won't necessarily agree with everything you say."

To be effective, consultants must be able to offer independent judgment on what is best for the business. Overall trust in the consultation process increases when the rest of the family realizes that the consultant is on no one individual's "side." The consultant is there to look out for the well-being of the family and the business. If you are deeply disappointed the first time the consultant disagrees with you in a meeting, you may not be fully aware of your hidden agenda in hiring the consultant.

Clients often unconsciously "transfer" to the consultant feelings and images derived from earlier relationships with family members like parents and siblings. Such fantasies can affect the process in powerful ways. Ideally, consultants are trained to be aware of this phenomenon and know how to work with it. You don't want a surrogate mother or a brother as a consultant, you want someone who can help you move your business into the future and ensure its health. By working with and raising awareness of transference at opportune times in the process, a skillful consultant can help the family business move into the future. However, not all professionals advising family businesses are specifically trained to pay attention to these dynamics.

The consultant, in turn, must be alert for signs of "counter-transference"—the dynamics of the consultant's own family of origin are likely to color his or her view of the client's family. Obviously, being trained to work with these dynamics is no guarantee of immunity from them.

So where does this leave the business owner? You can get some insight into them by monitoring your own reactions to the person you hire.

The first meeting with a consultant often provides abundant clues to your hidden assumptions. When people meet for the first time, they have little information about each other and tend to fill in the gaps with their own wishes and expectations for the relationship. After the first meeting with a consultant, ask yourself questions like: Why do I want to bring in a consultant? What do I envision the consultant doing for me personally and for our family business? What assumptions am I and others in my family making about this consultant? Am I inadvertently withholding information or doing anything else that might sabotage the process? Does the consultant seem to be leveling with me? Do I feel I can discuss these issues openly with the consultant? The answers to these questions can provide useful clues to some of your hidden assumptions.

The consulting process is unlikely to succeed without a realistic assessment, from the start, of what can and cannot be accomplished. When consultant and client have congruent expectations, when both are alert to the hidden assumptions and wishes that may affect the process, their relationship stands a good chance of being productive. The willingness and ability of both sides to talk about these issues as they arise may very well be the key to success.

— *Ivan Lansberg*

When to use a consultant

All kinds of people call themselves family business consultants these days. An expert panel offers advice on how to tell who's qualified and who's not, who's to be trusted and who's not.

THE RISE OF THE FAMILY BUSINESS consultant has been baffling to many business owners who might want professional help but are puzzled about just what a family business consultant does and how to find one who is qualified and right for their family.

Below, top consultants, family business experts, and owners help answer these questions. Their advice is distilled from a 1994 panel discussion held by *Family Business* magazine. The experts include Thomas Davidow, a psychologist and co-founder of Genus Resources; Nancy Bowman Upton, founder of the Institute for Family Business at Baylor University; Dirk Dreux IV, director of private business advisory services for United States Trust Company; Charles Fradin, president of Copley Distributors; Ernesto Poza, president of his own consulting firm, E.J. Poza Associates.

Q. What kind of service does a family business consultant provide and how does it differ from what a management consultant offers?

A. To some degree, family business consultants can be defined by the tasks they perform. For example, they work with clients to address ownership and management issues as well as family issues. They may deal with questions of succession, authority and business responsibility, job descriptions and compensation. The difference is that a family business consultant has to be able to look at the whole without having a conflict of interest. When a consultant is called on, the family is usually working through some type of trust or estate-related set of questions, which are inevitably tied to inter-generational kinds of issues. Somebody is going to leave the stage at some point, so that leads to questions about retirement planning. And, ultimately, the question arises: Okay, where is the liquidity going to come from to accomplish all this? A consultant understands the family system and the business system, and can analyze and treat both. It can be an individual or a team. In that sense, a lawyer, a banker, or an accountant does not qualify as a family business consultant.

Q. Are there people with different backgrounds and skills claiming to be family business consultants? You can't blame a business owner for being a little confused.

A. All the professional service firms that are trying to break into this market. One business owner complained that a guy came to him claiming to be a family business consultant and just wanted to sell him an insurance policy. It's very important for a client to find out how somebody gets paid. The person should be very straightforward about any conflicts of interest.

The best way for clients to inform themselves about a consultant—even after checking references—is to develop the relationship gradually. The best way for a client to find out whether the "fit" is right is to work right from the start on a specific problem that is concerning the client at that time. Instead of just having a polite converstion, the clients, in effect, get a chance to "kick the tires." If you feel you've gotten your money's worth from that first meeting, there is the possibility of an effective consultant-client relationship.

Q. What is the most common reason that family business owners seek the services of a consultant?

A. When they are having a problem in their relationships. Rarely do they call to ask for help in solving a problem with cash flow or financing and the like.

Q. Do you need to be a psychologist in order to be family business consultant?

A. If you are not a psychologist, or don't have a psychologist on your team, you are playing with fire. There should be an initial assessment of what is going on in the family—the family dynamics—and a thorough due diligence on the business issues. Then analyze how these two systems interact to produce the stress that the family is going through as a result of the tremendous amount of ambivalence in both systems.

Q. Where do family business consultants draw the line between what they do and therapy?

A. The work is therapeutic to the degree that the consultant attempts to create a healthy, safe environment in which people can talk about issues that are difficult. Often the issues are very similar to those that are discussed in a therapeutic situation. But the amount of time a consultant spends on such issues is quantifiably smaller. If the personal issues are interfering with the business, it is fine to discuss them. However, if you are stuck on them, it is time to make an additional referral so people can go someplace where they can get help with their personal issues.

Q. Can the company or family lawyer or accountant do what the family business consultant does?

A. No. They have usually been around so long that they're part of the system at this point. The new intervenor in the system can ask naive questions that the other people do not think to ask, or think they've been over this ground before and it's a closed issue for them.

Q. Is it important when hiring a consultant for the person to have some background in the client's industry?

A. Not necessarily. It can be especially useful for the clients to have to articulate for the consultant what their business is all about. Sometimes this is the first time anyone has forced them to do this. The answers to some very fundamental questions can be very revealing.

However, it does help for the person to be able to assimilate the language and terminology of the industry quickly and to understand how some companies measure the bottom line. There are significant differences between working with a company in the supermarket industry, for example, and working for an auto parts manufacturer that sells 80 percent of its products to the three major automotive companies. The client ought to be concerned about whether the consultant has the breadth and ability to understand what makes his or her industry tick.

Picking the best advisor

First, build a family consensus on what the problem is. Then put prospective consultants through their paces.

MANY FAMILY BUSINESSES look for outside help when dealing with interpersonal conflicts that become business problems. And a growing band of people who call themselves advisors are all too happy to service them, for fees that frequently reach several thousand dollars a day.

Because fees are so high and licensing is nonexistent, it's not surprising that family business consulting has attracted its share of the good, the bad, and the ugly. For a company in distress, survival may depend on the ability to distinguish between the highly skilled consultants and those whose primary interest is in financing their second home on Hilton Head.

Here are some guidelines to ensure your family gets the best help available.

Define the problem, in writing. If you can't write it down, you are not prepared to face it.

Build a family consensus. Your family must acknowledge that a problem exists and be willing to accept outside help. Reaching a consensus to seek help is often a gradual process. It might require some one-on-one politicking. Take family members to a seminar on family business at a nearby university, or get them to read books or periodicals that discuss family business problems. If they overcome their feelings of isolation, they'll start to see patterns, themes, and issues at the company that need to be resolved.

Seek referrals. Ask other family businesses, your lawyer, accountant, or other professionals for prospects. Check with local universities to see if they have family business programs. If you have attended a university program, look up some of the other attendees you met. Check with your industry association. Find out if there is a family business network in your city or region and talk with people there. The Family Firm Institute in Boston may be able to give you a list of people in your area with the specific expertise to address your problem.

Write to prospective advisors. Describe your company and the general problem, and invite their interest. Ask for their qualifications, how soon they can begin, and an indication of cost. Before meeting a candidate, ask him to submit, in writing, his assessment of the problem and his recommendations. Beware of any consultant who promises you the moon, or guarantees results.

Evaluate the responses, put together a short list, and start interviewing the candidates. At the interview, have your spouse present and any other family members crucial to the business. It helps avoid the feeling that the consultant is being brought in by one family member and is on that member's side. The consultant must be viewed as neutral, otherwise he cannot be effective. It should also be clear that there is no conflict of interest—that the advisor is not selling you something else, legal services for instance, in addition to the family advisory services.

You should be confident in an advisor's skills and sensitivity to the issues—and a high level of personal chemistry should exist between all parties.

Check references. This is probably the single most important way to verify an advisor's competence.

Family business issues are multi-dimensional. Many troubled firms require both the skills of a psychologist and the expertise of an estate planner. You should seek advisors who can marshall both the technical skills, such as law or finance, needed to deal with business, and the interpersonal skills needed to deal with families.

Does the advisor have experience in dealing with situations like yours? Don't let claims of confidentiality dissuade you from insisting on speaking with some previous family clients who had similar problems.

Study the advisor's initial proposal. Be sure it is specific. If you don't understand something, ask questions, especially about fees. There should be complete disclosure of the fee structure, whether it is a flat fee, hourly, daily, or weekly, and how expenses are to be handled. Follow the formal proposal with a letter of agreement so there is something in writing with which to resolve any future questions.

Do not base your decision strictly on price. Though fees range widely, they are all high. One advisor reportedly gets up to $20,000 per day. Other specialists command up to $3,000, and lesser lights charge $1,000. It will seem expensive, but how much do bad situations cost? It's not much use to haggle; consultants are usually firm on rates. If you want an ongoing retainer relationship, however, you might be able to get a break. Be sure to ask other questions related to cost such as anticipated expenses.

— *Louis Moscatello*

Picking the best attorney

Five experts discuss the qualities present in exceptional family business lawyers, and how to find the one best suited to your needs.

THE LEGAL PROFESSION IS LEARNING to appreciate the special skills and sensitivities required to serve family business clients.

When hiring outside counsel, owners are advised to look for training and experience in succession planning and other needs of family firms. Below, top family business experts and lawyers, who were gathered for a panel discussion by *Family Business* magazine, answer questions that will help owners choose the best attorney for their needs. The experts are Richard Narva, co-founder of Genus Resources; Bonnie Brown, director of the Institute for Family Business at Baylor University; Joe Goodman, an attorney with Holton Howard & Goodman P.C.; John Powell, a consultant with Nova Resources and former president of his family's business; and Robert Richards Jr., a partner with Hale and Dorr.

Q. What makes a good family business attorney?

A. He or she must definitely have broad skills and experience. They have to be process-oriented and recognize that solutions must be win-win and not have winners and losers. Lastly, they have to be truly empathetic and care about the family as well as the family business. They have to be more relationship-oriented than lawyers learn to be in law school. In many cases the most effective family business attorney is an older, mature individual.

Q. What types of questions should an owner ask in

order to determine whether an attorney is suited to working with his family business?

A. Potential clients should ask questions like: What percentage of your practice is with family or privately held businesses? How many of your lawyers have some training in and understanding of family systems? What makes your firm specifically suited to working with a family business? The family has to ask penetrating questions about the lawyer's specific experiences with succession and other family systems issues.

Most business owners are going to ask questions of a general nature, to build a profile of the lawyer and determine whether they can trust the person. They are more interested in building trust than in asking a lot of technical questions. They won't do business with the lawyer unless they like him as an individual.

Q. How should a family business owner go about hiring an attorney?

A. Outside references are very important. You have to find other family business owners who have worked with the attorney and like him or her. Usually family business owners are not just looking for someone to do an estate plan or write a will. They tend to stay with the attorney for a long period of time. So the relationship is important. You might find it helpful to consult *Martindale & Hubbell*, a directory which has a lot of information on lawyers' training and expertise.

Q. When a lawyer is engaged by a family business, who is considered the client?

A. There are, in effect, two roles that an attorney can play. One is an advocacy role, in which the lawyer is clearly representing a business and perhaps the owner. In those cases he has to make it understood that he is not representing the other family members and perhaps even suggest that they should be represented by other attorneys.

The second role would be that of a counselor to the entire family. In this case, the lawyer might be there simply to guide the family in a process—for example, if they are planning to engage a management consultant or a therapist to help them reduce some tension or conflict in the family. He is engaged to provide counsel to facili-

Sample questions to ask when hiring a lawyer

Is the attorney a generalist?

The family business owner should be looking for an attorney with broad experience, who has served family businesses and takes pride in "relationship lawyering." Specialists in one field of law, such as corporate, taxation, estate and probate, may not be qualified.

How will the attorney deal with conflicts between family members that may arise in the course of serving the family business?

The attorney should demonstrate that he or she has thought about situations in which conflicts arise in family businesses—as they often do. The candidate should acknowledge that, from a practical as well as ethical standpoint, he or she cannot represent both parties to a conflict. He or she should also be willing to recommend qualified professionals, if necessary, to help resolve family conflicts.

Does the attorney have the experience and personality to facilitate a

family system consulting process?

Look for signs that the attorney has the patience—and stomach—to help resolve disputes in the family rather than looking for quick, standardized solutions. Does the candidate seem to have the personality and experience to serve in a "process role" instead of the "advocacy role" to which most of their profession are accustomed?

How does the attorney propose that the business owner deal with the question of control of the company in the event of the owner's death or disability?

The attorney's answer should demonstrate sensitivity to the family issues that are involved in dividing and transferring ownership. Should the surviving spouse be given control until a successor in the next generation is ready to take charge? How will the division of stock between children who are active in the business and those who are not active affect their relationships?

Should the buy-sell agreement among family shareholders call for a high price reflecting the fair market value of the company if it is ever sold? Or should the price be low to facilitate gift and estate tax planning?

The answer should include an analysis of the benefits and drawbacks of each strategy. It should also show a concern for the financial situations of the different family members and their different perspectives.

What will be the legal costs of developing and implementing a shareholders' buy-sell agreement for my family business?

If an attorney weighs in with a low-ball estimate—say, $1,000 to $2,000—you should probably look for someone else. Any lawyer who has experience in drawing up these kinds of agreements for a family business will know that, in almost all cases, a great deal of time and expense will be required to do the job right. Costs of $4,000 to $8,000 are not uncommon.

tate a process, not to achieve results.

That, of course, requires informed consents and permissions from each family member, since the traditional attorney-client privilege is, if not waived, at least compromised. Instead of representing individual interests, the lawyer is looking toward the betterment of the entire family and the business.

Q. Is it possible for a lawyer to be an advocate for a member of the family one day and a counselor to the whole group the next?

A. It is hard to wear both hats. The problem is that sometimes the family business attorney enters a relationship with a client in the counselor's role, and the owner at some later time then asks the attorney to assume an advocacy role. If the attorney refuses, the owner feels betrayed. This goes back to trust. To be effective, the attorney has to be trusted by the entire family. He or she should bring up these issues from the very beginning of the engagement, so they are fully explored beforehand.

Q. Is a family business better off with a large law firm, a small firm, or a sole practitioner?

A. Some owners think the firm should be relatively large, so that the attorney will feel free to refer the client to areas of specialty within the firm. A large law firm that has a family business boutique within it can be ideal. Unfortunately, a lot of law firms don't have family business practice groups. So when an owner makes contact with an attorney in the firm, there's no telling what kind of background he or she will have. The attorney could be an estate lawyer or a specialist in contracts. Usually the person will be a business attorney, because that's what the owner wants to talk about.

Others believe the relationship of the family business lawyer and the owner is so intimate that it doesn't make any difference whether the person comes from a large firm or a small firm, as long as the attorney is professional and diligent. A lawyer in a small firm can develop relationships with large firms and hand off work that he is unable to do.

Q. How do lawyers tend to charge family business clients?

A. Twenty years ago attorneys were given a retainer for representing the family and the business, and they and the owners worked out charges for specific work that both agreed were reasonable. Charges were billed on the basis of "fairness" for services rendered. Now, because of complaints about the quality of billing, clients tend to be billed by the hour. The result is that the business owner tries to keep discussions with their attorney focused on the legal issues. This tends to prevent the attorney from obtaining necessary background information on family issues.

In a perfect world, lawyers would be on retainer, so they wouldn't have to charge clients for routine phone calls. At times clients won't call because they don't want to get a bill for a 15-minute phone call. Some lawyers are using retainers to cover ongoing, routine matters, and then charge appropriately for project-type work.

How to rate your insurance company

Six key indices show whether or not an insurer will survive the long haul and be able to deliver what it promises. Use them to test your firm or find a new one.

WILL YOU OUTLIVE your life insurance company? Until quite recently, the question was rhetorical. Today, however, insurance companies are no more stable than banks. The industry's troubles can have a particularly strong impact on family business owners, who depend on insurance companies to fund stock repurchase agreements, wealth-transfer plans, and estate-tax liquidity needs.

In the past, a business owner could select an insurer, then stick with the choice for the long term. Today, such a hands-off approach could have disastrous consequences. To protect yourself, you need to research financial institutions—banks, thrifts, insurance carriers—as rigorously as those institutions examine persons applying for loans or insurance.

Monitoring the industry's members—in terms of both short-term performance and long-term survival—begins by checking credit rating agencies reports. Outfits such as A.M. Best, Moody's, Standard and Poor's, and Duff and Phelps analyze the finances of hundreds of insurers and pass judgment on the firms' financial health.

Credit-rating agencies provide a good overview. For more detailed information, business owners should ask their accountants to investigate six key indices that measure an insurer's ability to meet its projected returns.

1. A rule of thumb for evaluating an insurer's financial strength involves its level of capital and surplus—the amount of money above the reserves that the company is mandated by law to set aside. Insurers with assets of $1 billion to $10 billion should have capital and surplus equal to 5 percent to 10 percent of total assets. Firms with assets in excess of $10 billion should have capital and surplus of

3 percent to 7 percent of total assets. Moreover, capital and surplus should grow by at least 5 percent annually.

2. An insurer's mortality experience—the pricing of products based on average life expectancies—should earn a "most favorable" or "very favorable" rating from a credit rating service. A poorer rating suggests that an insurer has made incorrect assumptions about mortality averages, which can narrow its profit margin, forcing the company either to increase its policy charges or reduce its surplus.

3. Examine the quality of an insurer's investment portfolio. Be cautious if a rating agency such as Standard and Poor's or Moody's reports that a company keeps more than 10 percent of its assets in junk bonds or nonperforming real estate loans. Risky investments may generate high yields, but they also can plummet in a flash.

4. Check the yields of a company's investments. Most insurers guarantee yields of no more than 5.5 percent but often pay twice that amount. Today, those high-end yields are depressed, and policyholders who thought they'd receive a 13 percent return throughout the life of their policy are hopping mad. Make sure your insurer is offering a credible rate. And beware of a company that projects a higher rate than the rate it's earning on its own investments.

5. Track your carrier's expense ratio. The expense of administering policies is difficult to evaluate since insurers sometimes hide these charges in other areas of the business. Annual credit service expenses during a five-year period should average no more than 5 percent of premium income plus policy reserves.

6. Check the number of individuals who let their policies lapse at a specific carrier. When the so-called lapse rate is low (10 percent or less), a company can price its products quite competitively because it has a good chance of recovering its initial investment through continuing premiums paid by policyholders.

Finally, don't make the mistake of placing more emphasis on the policy than the insurance company. Look for the healthiest carrier, and then get the policy that best suits your needs. Don't blindly place all of your insurance eggs in one basket; diversifying your policies among several insurers is the safest hedge against an uncertain economy.

— *Mike Cohn*

Picking the best insurance agent

Once you've identified solid insurance companies, it's time to pick an agent. A checklist of key criteria will enable you to select the best one from a sea of choices.

L IFE INSURANCE is almost always an important part of an estate plan for family business owners. Yet many owners devote little attention to selecting a qualified life insurance agent. Too often, they choose on the basis of price and premium considerations alone. Typically, the agent selected is the person nearest at hand— a golfing partner, the agent who handles the family's home or automobile policy, a nephew who has begun work in a life insurance company.

This casual, haphazard approach to the purchase of life insurance is dangerous considering you are buying a product that must be monitored over time and may not pay off for decades. In these cases, policies receive inadequate attention as the needs of the family and the business change, and both end up short of the necessary liquidity to cover their needs after a death. It is much

Credit-rating services that examine insurers

To determine *whether your insurance company is fiscally fit, review its credit ratings reports. Ask you agent for reports from A.M. Best, Standard and Poor's, Moody's, and Duff and Phelps, or purchase reports on your own.*

● A. M. Best Company. Reports $15. Ambest Road, Oldwick, NJ 08858; 201-439-2200.

● Standard & Poor's Insurance Rating Services. Analysis of carriers' claims-paying ability. Reports $25. 25 Broadway, New York, NY 10004; 212-208-8000.

● Moody's Investors Service. Rates the financial condition of life insurance companies, similar to its bond-rating system. Reports cost $1,050 annually; summaries cost $125 per year. 99 Church Street, New York, NY 10007; 212-553-1658.

● Duff & Phelps. Rates the claims-paying ability of life insurers. Reports for varying fees. 55 E. Monroe Street, Chicago IL 60603; 312-263-2610.

● National Association of Insurance Commissioners. Sells reports which track companies that have fallen outside its own five measures of risk. Fee is $50. 120 W. 12th Street, Suite 1100, Kansas City, MO 64015; 816-842-3600.

● The American Bar Association. Publishes the ABA Primer: Life Insurance Products, Illustrations, and Due Dilligence. Costs $34.95 plus $3.95 for shipping. 750 N. Lakeshore Drive, Chicago, IL 60611; 312-988-5571.

wiser to use a more careful, systematic approach, which includes the following:

First, know your needs. Life insurance can take care of various cash needs precipitated by death, including payment of estate taxes; income for a spouse or other dependent family members; funding a stock purchase under a buy-sell agreement; strengthening the company balance sheet to overcome the loss of a key executive. It is important to scope out what your needs will be and attach projected numbers to them.

Second, select one agent for the whole family. Though some family members may prefer to have their own agent, all can obtain a higher level of service if the family unit can agree on selection of one qualified professional. Choosing one agent to handle the needs of everyone is particularly important when several family members work in a business and coverage must be coordinated with company coverage. It avoids costly and time-consuming duplication in the work of the company's advisory team and ensures greater confidentiality, since only one person and not several is entrusted with sensitive financial information.

Third, ask the person you expect to use to review your current policies and to compare them with alternative products available in the marketplace. Life insurance policies vary in type and quality. It is extremely important to monitor their performance regularly and update them if necessary. An assessment of your current policies and how they stack up can be a good test of the kind of service you can expect from the agent you're planning to use.

Fourth, the likelihood of getting the family to agree on one agent is enhanced when the members develop criteria for what they want in an agent beforehand. Having agreed-upon criteria helps family members formulate questions that should be asked in the screening process and to reach consensus on the best-qualified candidate. No one agent will satisfy all of the criteria, and some will be more important to you than others.

A Life Insurance Agent Checklist that spells out the criteria should include the following items:

Age and experience. It costs the same to hire an experienced agent as an inexperienced one. The person you choose should have specialized for at least 10 years in life insurance for professionals, executives, and family businesses. Age becomes an issue if you are a younger person with long-term insurance needs; because you will want someone who can service your policy over a life-

Choose one agent for the family. It decreases duplication of work and increases confidentiality.

time, you may not want to deal with an agent who is close to retirement.

Life insurance company affiliations. Agents that specialize in other types of insurance—such as property or casualty—can gain access to life insurance companies through qualified life insurance agents and brokers. Agents who don't work directly with the companies are, in general, less desirable because they don't have a direct relationship with these companies and are likely to be less experienced in the life area.

In addition, the agent you choose should represent several large life insurance companies, well-known for products in the professional, executive, and family business marketplace. It is unrealistic to expect one company to provide the best product for your every life insurance need.

Size of the agency. The agent should be affiliated with an established and well-known agency, or with an independent insurance and financial planning group in your local area. When you go with a smaller agency or group, you face the possibility that it may one day go out of business, because of competition from larger companies or adverse economic circumstances, leaving you with "orphan" policies that do not receive close attention and proper service.

Back-office support staff. Many of the best agencies and financial planning groups have staff members in your local area who can monitor your policies on a regular basis and provide continuing advice on alternative products. Other agencies rely on staff support from regional or national offices, which means you have less chance of receiving prompt information or service.

Satisfied customers. Any agent who wants your business should be able to provide a list of clients as well as professionals such as accountants and lawyers with whom he or she has worked in the past. Don't hesitate to call these references for any agent whom you anticipate using. Ideally, the list should include family business clients with needs similar to yours.

Success factor. Evidence of continued financial success and prosperity should be one criterion for selecting an agent. Agents who don't show evidence of consistent success may suddenly decide to change careers, leaving you, once again, with orphaned policies. In contrast, a career agent who has been financially successful is more likely to be patient and feel less pressure to sell you a lot of insurance you may not need.

Compatibility. The level of comfort you feel with the

person is important. Much of this comfort comes from having common interests and values. You will work with this person for years. Find out what you can about the agent's personal background and interests—ethnic group, place of worship, schools, family, neighborhood, social and service club affiliations, hobbies.

Team player. The agent you choose will have to work closely with other members of your advisory team. Beware of those who claim to be experts on almost anything—especially things outside their specialty, such as drawing up wills, estate planning, and cash flow. They may clash with your lawyer, accountant,or banker.

Finally, listen closely to what insurance agents think is important and the kinds of information they volunteer. The agent will be in contact with you and your family at critical junctures in your lives. Sensitivity to and experience with family issues and concerns can vital at these times. One of the best clues to whether the agent is right for your family business is whether the person reveals this sensitivity in the initial interview, without questions or prodding from you.

— Joe M. Goodman

— VI —

SUCCESSION

SUCCESSION is a process that takes decades, encompassing everything from how children are inspired and trained to take over the business to financial strategies for passing on the most ownership for the least estate taxes. And as a process, it must be properly managed if it is to succeed.

Succession activities also strongly affect the operation of the company, and vice versa. This interaction must be managed as well.

A key step is to involve all the major stakeholders, to reach consensus about how succession will take place and how executives will handle the stresses the process will create. Completion of the 12 key tasks in Chapter 23 will ensure a smooth transition.

Inevitably, certain top nonfamily employees will feel compelled to leave after realizing they have no chance at the top spot. If you want them to stay, you can offer them equity—or try one of the incentives explained in Chapter 24, that won't dilute family ownership.

Mentoring is critical to the success of the incoming leader. Chapter 25 explains how to carry out the mentoring process so the company's top executives accept the leadership change and their new roles.

Having carefully orchestrated the succession process, owners can finally retire. But problems can develop later. Owners should protect their retirement income with a number of legal and financial stipulations on the firm and successors, as described in the last chapter. These don't imply lack of trust…just smart planning.

Twelve Tasks in Succession

Build consensus, pick a candidate, and define roles

Orderly completion of 12 key tasks will help ensure a smooth transition and aid the family in defining the products, services, and markets for which the business is best suited.

ON A CONSCIOUS LEVEL, most owner-managers know that succession planning is the right thing to do, for their families and the business. But emotional forces are tugging in the opposite direction, often preventing them from facing the issues. If a consultant is involved, he or she can work to overcome these resistances and strengthen the forces in favor of planning by guiding the family toward a vision of the future that all can accept; by helping them create a step-by-step plan for getting there that allows all to accustom themselves to their new roles gradually; and by constantly reminding them of the consequences of doing no planning.

The complexity of the process, of course, depends on what type of ownership and management structure the firm has had in the past and what type it is moving toward for the future. Three fundamental forms of family businesses have been identified: the owner-managed company, the sibling partnership, and the cousin syndicate. These types are not necessarily sequential. Not all firms are started and run by a single entrepreneur. A group of siblings who founded a company and ran it as equal partners may decide that the best structure for the second generation would be a single owner-manager.

Whatever structure the owners and key stakeholders decide they want, however, they must accomplish 12 specific tasks during continuity planning.

1. Decide whether the family wants to continue ownership. This basic decision is extremely difficult to discuss and is typically avoided. For many families, the business is an important vehicle for family connectedness—the primary hub around which family life revolves. The older generation's deep attachment to the firm makes it difficult for them to think about the alternatives of selling or liquidating. Even talking about the family's commitment to the business is like questioning the members' love and respect for one another.

But continuity requires that those who will be in charge of the company's future develop a firm commitment to the business and to one another. For this to happen, stakeholders must understand the reasons that it is in their interest to maintain family ownership. They must make an informed choice.

2. Assess whether the family can withstand the stresses that continuity planning inevitably generates. It's not enough for the family to decide that it wants to stay in the business. The members also have to understand that the planning process will at times be painful, and that when it is finished, not everyone may be satisfied by the result.

Continuity planning requires conversations that even the healthiest families would much rather avoid. It involves openly discussing such issues as aging, death, and inheritance. It requires making hard decisions about distributing economic assets among loved ones, and it may involve giving favored positions to some siblings and cousins over others. Above all, it leads to wrenching changes that demand new ways of coping.

Leaders must assess whether their family has the characteristics needed to succeed at planning. It's up to the leaders to decide whether they should put the family—and themselves—through a process that may, in some cases, be divisive and leave bitter feelings.

3. Get the owner-manager(s) to agree to actively manage the development of a continuity plan and the transition in leadership to the next generation. It is often those without power in a business who call on consultants for help with succession. Without the support of the principal owner-manager, however, the process is usually doomed to fail. And the owner-manager must not only agree to come to terms with letting go; he must also agree to actively manage the design and implementation of the plan.

By getting him to make that commitment, you increase the odds that the owner will buy into the process at each stage and use his power to see that the plan is carried out. Once the owner-manager has announced that he will step down by a certain date, for example, the process gains a certain momentum, which also makes it extremely difficult for the owner to change his mind.

Help a successor gain authority by publicly communicating trust in his abilities.

4. Consult and actively involve other major stakeholders in the process. The views of those whose lives will be affected by the plan—key family members, senior managers, stockholders—should be solicited whenever possible. Their support will be necessary to carrying out the plan. They should be informed about what the planning entails, the frequency and format of the meetings, items on the agenda, and so on.

Senior managers may have valuable information about the impact of the plan on various constituencies such as customers and employees. The senior managers' views on strategic considerations in the plan are also essential.

Members of the next generation must, of course, have an opportunity to express their views and to influence decisions. They should not be kept in the dark about important matters such as how ownership of the enterprise will be divided under the parent's estate plan.

Though the planning process should be truly consultative, it need not be democratic. Lines of authority should be respected, and parents should retain their right to make the final decisions.

5. Set up appropriate forums for reaching consensus on key issues. At least three structures should be developed: a family council for discussion of family issues; a board of directors (if the company doesn't already have one) to deal with ownership and policy issues; and a succession task force to elaborate the strategic aspects of the plan and assist in the training of the successors.

The family council is the place to discuss such matters as the wishes and needs of individual members, the values they share, and whether they want to perpetuate the firm. It provides a setting where differences can be aired and worked through without interfering with the daily management of the business.

To empower the board, the company should appoint at least three top-notch outsiders as directors. Structurally, the board's role is to design policies that protect the family's wishes and values. The board can also provide badly needed perspective and expertise during continuity planning, provided it is not beholden to the owner-manager or one faction in the company. (In one firm that I studied, the founder explicitly charged his board with the task of alerting him to any unconscious attempts on his part to undermine the design and implementation of a succession plan.)

The mission of the succession task force is to develop a five-year strategic plan for the business and to define the qualities needed in future leaders who will carry out that plan. The task force identifies a list of senior manager candidates and prescribes the further training each needs to sharpen his or her skills and knowledge of the business. Besides the owner-manager, the task force should include one or two nonfamily senior managers and the leading successor candidates.

6. Develop a clear vision for the future of the business that all key family members can enthusiastically share and that spells out the role each will play. The roles of family members can be defined by picturing three circles, representing family, ownership, and management, which intersect in places. Each member participates in one or more of the circles. Owner-managers are usually leaders in all three.

Family members have to be able to visualize what their company is going to look like five years from now, how their roles are going to change, and what these shifts in power and influence imply for both the family and the business. After succession, the owner-manager, for example, is no longer at the center of management but may perhaps remain an owner. He or she and other family members thus have to be able to envision how that will change their relationship.

Along with trying to imagine how roles will change, the family must develop a strategic vision of the firm's future. It is important to ask such questions as: What kind of business do we want to have in the future? In what kinds of markets will we be operating? What kinds of products and services will we offer? Once the family agrees on a future scenario, the leaders can work toward achieving a good fit between that vision and the interests and skills of members of the next generation.

A vision requires much more than being able to imagine various future alternatives, however. It involves getting the family to define the hopes and dreams that they share for the business. Members of the older and younger generations must agree on why it is significant to be in the business, why it is an activity worth perpetuating.

The vision may be left vague, so that all can hook their dreams to it. Usually, it implies a social mission beyond profit-making. The business is seen as playing a significant role in the welfare of its employees or the community. The leaders see themselves (in the phrase used by John Ward of Loyola University) as "stewards of capital" who are responsible for preserving the firm and carrying on its good works until it is passed on to a new generation. Without such a shared vision, it is doubtful that continuity planning can be sustained.

7. Choose a successor and other candidates for the future top management team, and plan a course of training for each. After developing a strategic vision, the next question becomes: What kind of leadership is needed to successfully perform under this scenario?

The management task force should make a list of the managerial, technical, and personal skills they consider critical for the next generation. Then the task force should identify potential candidates for the top leadership positions. A common error at this stage is to assume that a person who has not done well in one job is not capable of exceptional work in any number of other future jobs. Young people are learning and growing and should not be counted out too soon.

The key here is to design effective training and work experiences so that those identified as having leadership ability can acquire the skills they need and have opportunities to prove their mettle. To fully assess their potential, they must be given real jobs with accountability and measurable performance standards.

8. Help the successor build authority both in the family and in the business. A continuity plan provides for the transfer of power and authority. The distinction between the two is subtle but important. Power refers to a person's capacity to influence the behavior of others. Authority, by contrast, refers to a person's right to influence others, meaning that his or her power is regarded by others as legitimate.

Successors in family businesses often get jobs that give them power before they have earned the authority that comes with perceived competence in the eyes of employees. Owner-managers can help successors gain authority by publicly supporting them and communicating trust in their abilities. (Of course, owner-managers can also hinder successors by signaling a lack of confidence in them.) But basically successors must earn respect on their own, through their educational attainments, through their performance inside and outside the company, and by demonstrating they have the long-term interests of the company and its employees at heart.

Since the head of the business inevitably has great influence within the family, the successor must also win the respect of family members by demonstrating trustworthiness and a commitment to protecting the interests of all.

9. Design an estate plan that specifies how ownership of the enterprise will eventually be distributed among members of the next generation. In too many families, the business owner plans his estate with lawyers, and family members learn the details only after the owner's death. That can lead to misinterpretations of the real intentions of the parent and to bitterness among heirs.

Discussing the plan with the beneficiaries ahead of time gives parents the opportunity to explain their reasons for dividing up the estate in a particular way. In some cases, they may decide to alter the plan after these discussions in order to ensure future family harmony. By letting members of the next generation know what they can expect to inherit, moreover, the parents enable them to plan their lives accordingly, based on realistic expectations of their inheritance.

10. Make sure family members understand the rights and responsibilities that come with the various roles they will assume. While much attention is given to the management training of successors, other family members are usually less well prepared for their ownership roles. For example, people who own stock but do not participate in the business are often frustrated by their lack of influence. Family stockholders should be able to ask well-informed questions of management about the financial state of the business, provided they go through appropriate channels. They also need to appreciate the fundamental distinction between ownership and management. For that, they need instruction.

Likewise, those in management may need a refresher course in their obligations to stockholders. Often the managers assume that those who are not involved in the business have no legitimate claim to share in its profits.

Design strategies for informing customers, suppliers, and creditors about the plan.

Retiring owner-managers may also benefit from some instruction. For example, the owner who has been directly involved in day-to-day operations for years and now plans to teach part-time at a local business college is likely to need coaching in what it takes to be a successful classroom teacher.

11. Inform important stakeholders—customers, suppliers, creditors—about the firm's continuity plan. The objective here is to reduce any uncertainty about the future of the business. Family firms tend to be overly secretive, not realizing the extent of their dependence on the external environment. Obviously, outsiders do not need to know about internal debates over succession issues; the continuity plan must be discussed and carefully developed before the details are publicly disclosed. But disclosure is essential to managing the firm's relations with business constituencies and the community.

The succession task force should first identify the various constituencies that need to be informed about the plan. Then the task force should develop a tailor-made strategy for informing each. The strategy should include systematic efforts to introduce the successors to these important outsiders and to connect them with influential government and community leaders.

Disclosing the timetable for succession to outsiders can also have internal benefits: It helps to keep the continuity plan on track. Once the details have been publicly disclosed, it becomes much more difficult for the owner-manager, or anyone else, to sabotage the process.

12. Develop a contingency succession plan, just in case. Carrying out a continuity plan may, as we have mentioned, take five years or more. In that time, emergencies can upset the best laid plans. The owner-manager could die unexpectedly; so, in fact, could the chosen successor.

It is important to think about worst-case scenarios, and to spell out what would happen in the event of such developments. Like the continuity plan itself, the emergency plan should address ownership, management, and family considerations. For example, it might name an experienced nonfamily manager to take over as CEO until the owners can select and train a family successor. The plan might indicate how the ownership shares of the owner-manager should eventually be distributed. It might also call for the purchase of accident or "critical person" insurance to cover a significant portion of the business's debt.

These, then, are the 12 basic tasks of continuity planning. From this discussion, the overall characteristics of a successful continuity plan should be clear. First, the plan must be strategic; it must be based on a thorough analysis of future markets and the growth prospects of the business. Second, the plan must be comprehensive; it must acknowledge the complex interaction of family, ownership, and management issues. Third, the plan must be feasible; it must be based on a realistic assessment of what is attainable for both the family and the firm at a given juncture in their development. (The life-style expectations of the members, for example, cannot exceed the potential of the business for meeting them.)

Fourth and most important, the continuity plan must be managed; its design and implementation must be orchestrated by those with power to make the critical decisions. Managing the transition is the hard work of selecting the people and creating the structures necessary for moving a complex system from one generation to the next.
— *Ivan Lansberg*

Ensuring Stability During Transition

Incentives to keep nonfamily executives through succession

Top managers may leave if they are not given a piece of the action. There are several ways to provide equity incentives without losing any family control.

IN THE BEST OF ALL POSSIBLE WORLDS, the next generation is ready to take over the reins just as the older generation is letting go. But the world seldom works on cue. Often children are not yet seasoned enough to assume control. When that is the case, it is important to hang on to the key nonfamily managers to fill the void until the next generation is ready. One way to do this is to give them a "piece of the action," in a way that doesn't diminish family control.

Family business owners often reject this approach completely, seeing only a potential threat to future family ownership. What they fail to understand is that there are several ways to provide equity incentives to nonfamily members without risking any loss of family control. By tying additional rewards to long-term performance, the owner creates a "golden handcuff" that motivates valued managers to take a perspective that parallels the family's.

Consider Paul Jordan, owner of Jordan Supply, a (fictitious) $25 million wholesale plumbing business, who was approaching retirement. Although Paul wanted ownership to remain in family hands, he recognized that his two sons, both active sales managers for the company, still lacked the experience necessary to run the highly competitive business. However, Paul's general manager, Bill Galt, had the expertise necessary to guide the company in the interim. To bridge the gap until his sons were ready, Paul had to keep the loyalty of this talented employee.

Paul looked at stock options, either an incentive plan or a non-qualified plan and discussed phantom stock or cash bonuses. He decided on an inactive stock option plan, giving Bill the right to acquire nonvoting shares. This plan would give Bill the financial benefits and motivation he sought, plus favorable tax treatment. But by coupling the plan with a stock redemption program, family control would be protected, since Bill would have to sell his shares back to Jordon Supply when he reached retirement or terminated employment. But by using nonvoting common stock, Paul let Bill share in the company's growth.

An incentive stock option plan grants the participant an option to acquire shares in the company based on a predetermined price. An outside valuation determines the stock's fair market value, in this case, book value. The company then grants options to purchase the stock at this price to Bill. The grant of options is not a taxable event to the recipient.

After the grant of the options, any increase in the company's book value remains a tax-free benefit to Bill. Incentive stock options (ISOs) permit Bill to exercise the options any time within 10 years. When he does, he can purchase his shares at the original grant price, regardless of current fair market value. The purchase (exercise of the options) is not taxable.

Once he buys the shares, Bill must hold them for at least two years to qualify for capital gains treatment on their sale. If he qualifies, Bill will pay capital gains taxes on the difference between the price for which he sells the stock back to Jordan Supply and the grant price. (The two-year holding period is waived for Bill's heirs in the event of his death.) If Bill sells before the two-year period, he pays ordinary income tax on the difference between his sale price and the grant price. The company gets a deduction equal to Bill's income.

The companion stock redemption agreement lets the company repurchase Bill's shares at market value when he retires, is terminated, becomes disabled, or dies. If Bill is terminated and has not yet exercised the options, he will have one year to do so. He can then hold them for the two-year period to qualify for capital gains or put them back to the company immediately, in which case he incurs ordinary income taxes on the gains and the company gets a deduction. (If Paul were leery of letting a terminated man hold even nonvoting shares, he could have insisted on Bill exercising the options, paying Bill a cash bonus at termination equal to the income taxes Bill paid in excess of the capital gains rates.)

The current book value of Jordan Supply is $3 million or $3,000 per each of its 1,000 shares outstanding. Bill was granted options to acquire 30 shares worth $90,000. He plans to exercise his option eight years from now, and then sell those shares back to the company two years later, just before his retirement. His cost will still be $90,000. Assume the book value purchase rises 7 percent a year to $6,000 by the time Bill retires. The $180,000 Bill would receive represents a $90,0000 gain to be taxed at then-current capital gain rates.

The ISO plan gave Paul the missing link he needed for his own retirement. He already trusted Bill to run the company. Now as an "owner," Bill had additional incentive to protect Paul's interests as well as his own.

Bill's temporary "ownership" through the ISO plan does not conflict with Paul's long-term objective to keep the business in family hands or his hope that his sons would eventually be able to run the company. At some point, the company would have to be sure it had enough cash on hand to buy back Bill's shares.

If a company extends its ISO plan to family members, additional restrictions are imposed on those family participants. Options must be exercised at 110 percent, rather than 100 percent, of the stock's fair market value and they must be exercised within 5 years rather than 10. This can make them less attractive to family members.

What about alternatives to the ISO plan? Nonqualified stock options, phantom stock, or cash bonuses can be appropriate tools to motivate and hang on to nonfamily employees. Tax treatment on them however, is more favorable to the company than to the recipient.

Nonqualified options result in ordinary income taxes when the options are exercised rather than when they are sold. The amount taxed is the difference between the grant price and the fair market value on the date the options are exercised. The corporation gets a deduction equal to the income reported by the participant.

Phantom stock may be an attractive alternative. It is exactly what the name implies: no stock is transferred. Instead, participant is granted "appreciation rights" to a specified number of shares. The appreciation may be defined by a change in book value or by another measure of growth. Annual valuations provide a method of reporting the phantom stock's performance to the participant. The participant in a phantom stock plan is a general creditor of the company; the value of the appreciation rights is analogous to an accrued bonus. The appreciation rights are paid out on retirement, termination, death, or disability. They are taxed as ordinary income an are expensed by the company as paid.

Administrative costs of a phantom stock plan may be higher than an ISO plan due to the necessity for valuing and reporting appreciation rights annually.

If performance-oriented managers want to build their net worth now rather than defer it, owners may consider cash bonuses based on current performance and paid out as earned. But cash bonuses do not handcuff that essential employee, or provide any long-term incentives.

— *Mike Cohn*

The pros and cons of stock plans

	ISO plan	Non-qualified stock options	Phantom stock
Is employee taxed on purchase?	No	Yes	No
How is gain treated?	Capital gain	Ordinary income	Ordinary income
How are options and appreciation rights valued?	Fair market value	Any price set by board	Any price set by board
Are distributions to employee deductible?	No	Yes, equal to income reported by employee	Yes, equal to income reported by employee

Mentoring the Next Generation

Mentors must challenge their heirs to learn

Successful teaching requires all those who have a stake in the process to be prepared for their roles. Here's what owners, mentors, and successors should expect.

MENTORING the young son or daughter of a family business is treated much too casually by too many owners. Usually the kid just shows up one day in the office and is turned over to Old Joe, without any great thought having been given to what Joe ought to teach him or whether the chemistry between them will be right.

Parents who hope their children will one day enter the business and lead it into the future should begin education early on. Successful mentoring requires a long warmup. It shouldn't be a two-week survey course in Daddy's business after which the kid becomes executive vice-president. And all of those who have a stake in the process—parents, children, spouses, siblings, and the mentors themselves—have to buy into the idea and be prepared for their part in it. Otherwise, it's not likely to be very effective.

Parents create the clay with which the mentor will have to work. When the children are growing up, the parents should expose them to heroes—to great coaches, great teachers, great adults they can look up to, people who exemplify values that the parents and society endorse. When children grow up feeling that employees of their father's company are their domestics, when they are led to believe that they are entitled to rule, when what is "right" in their opinion is not subject to review, they are unlikely to listen to any mentor. If Dad has been accustomed to bad-mouthing his employees at home, if he's always talking about how they lie and steal from him, any employee who's later given the job of mentoring starts with two strikes against him.

The mentor, for his part, is asked to assume a heavy burden, with many attendant risks. He is being asked to tutor a young person who may gradually annex his responsibilities and perks, who someday will be his boss.

Others may have a stake as well in the mentor's approach and opinions. For example, the same mentor is often asked to teach several of the boss's kids, in which case he is likely to be eventually asked his opinion on the choice of a successor in the business. The owner's opinion can be different than that of his spouse; instead of helping to pick one leader that all can support, the mother may want their children to share leadership and responsibilities. Mentors become "men in the middle." The temptation, when asked for an opinion, is to waffle: "Well, they are all smart and working hard..."

Ideally, children and potential mentors should get to know each other well before the kids show up at the company. Parents should occasionally bring their senior managers and trusted advisors to family dinners. They should take the children on visits to the plant and office, where their potential successors can get to know and respect those who will be passing on valuable knowledge. When the chemistry is right, these mentors will have a major role in the last stages of the children's upbringing.

Most often, mentoring works best when the teacher is much older and accepts that both his own future security and that of the firm are tied to his protégé's successful mastery of the necessary attitudes and skills.

When the age spread between mentor and student is too close, sparks often fly. Matching a 40-year-old sales manager with a 30-year-old son, for example, could be a disaster. If the two become rivals, Dad may have to choose between keeping a valued employee and teaching his son. The father may have to take the manager aside and say: "If you can't work with my son and prepare him for ultimate leadership of my company, you may prefer to leave now and find another job. There is no way you're going to be my successor, but your future can be assured as a mentor."

Mentors have to earn acceptance from their students. They should come to their responsibility with the attitude of "How can I help make this work well?" But successors also have to buy into the relationship, and understand that there is no appeal to a higher court. For once a mentor is accepted, his job is not to be a soft, pliable buddy. A successful family business is not a safe haven for incompetents. There are rules that have to be followed and tough decisions to be made. Discipline is a matter of survival. Mentors must insist on it.

What is to be learned? A lot. Over time, young successors-to-be should probably have a series of mentors, not just one—the senior vice-president for marketing, finance, and production, the firm's auditors, bankers, and attorneys, perhaps an outside consultant who has the right background and works well with young people.

It is up to these mentors to indicate which skills and attitudes their students must master.

A mentor must challenge heirs to learn what they must learn. But even more important, he must pass on to them the same sense of excitement, of joy, that both he and the founder-parent felt in building the business. Above all, he must help create leadership and a positive attitude toward this responsibility. The young student must earn credibility in the eyes of those who will be his followers.

Mentoring that really counts instills a sense of mission, an appreciation of strategy, an urge to contribute. Today, in too many companies, no one seems to have the heart to lead in these matters. The business owner is lonely and tired of fighting off the alligators snapping at his ankles. His advisors want to play it safe and avoid the big decisions. His senior managers want to be followers. Even his board doesn't want to think about the future.

But the new generation must think about the future of the business. The ultimate destiny of the company lies in their hands. A wise mentor with a clear vision will earn his glory through the accomplishments of his students.

— *Léon Danco*

The difference between parenting and mentoring

To be effective mentors, seniors must understand the differences between *parenting* and *mentoring*. Some get into difficulties because they insist on continuing to parent their adult offspring—sometimes until the offspring are well into the 50s! Others get into trouble because they try to mentor their children prematurely—a 10-year-old boy or girl needs a parent, not a mentor.

One of the secrets of an effective succession transition is finding an optimal blend of parenting and mentoring that is well timed developmentally.

Effective mentoring also requires an appropriate degree of *differentiation*—on both sides. Seniors cannot be effective mentors if they continue to see their adult offspring simply as younger versions of themselves. Juniors must be able to appreciate their parents virtues as well as their

shortcomings—neither idealization nor deprecation help.

Even the best of mentoring relationships typically do not last forever. They all come to an end once the mentee feels that he or she is capable of functioning independently. Often this happens when the mentee reaches his or her 40s, during the mid-life period.

The end of the mentoring relationships can be difficult—sometimes even traumatic. Negotiating the end is particularly tricky. It is one thing to part ways with a mentor to whom one is not related; it is quite another to cut off relations with a father, mother, uncle, aunt, or sibling.

In those family businesses in which a blow-up is avoided, the mentoring relationship usually continues overtly—by mutual consent—but without much further learning going

on. Mentor and mentee do a face-saving dance that allows them both to disagree graciously.

For parental mentoring to be effective the process must be negotiated with the juniors, right from the start, laying out specific jobs and competencies that need to be mastered at each stage before the mentee moves on to the next stage.

Juniors must be assigned real jobs that generate reliable performance data—it is the only way to help the juniors acquire authority. The career path must be designed with the future in mind—mentor for the business of the future, not the one you have today.

When mentoring is successful, parents and offspring are able to maintain love and mutual respect, while setting up real tests of the mentee's capabilities. — *Ivan Lansberg*

The nonfamily mentor's guide

Executives who are not related to potential heirs make the best mentors. Several tasks and techniques will help them carry out their mission.

THE EMOTIONAL TIES that bind families make it next to impossible for parents to provide career guidance to their own offspring. Or, for that matter, for the offspring to hear that advice in an unfiltered and open manner. One of the most valuable contributions a nonfamily executive can make in the family business is to facilitate the successful transition of the future chief executive. They should be ready and willing to become a mentor. But they may not be. And even if they are, they may not know how to carry out their duty.

The following is addressed to mentors: how they should see their role, and what they should do. Owners should understand the advice, too.

To function most effectively as a mentor, you should play a role in specifying the requirements for the successor's job; helping to identify and recommend the most appropriate successor when there is more than one potential family candidate; and coaching the successor so that he or she is fully prepared to assume the reins.

In establishing the criteria for management succession, you should evaluate both the current requirements of the position and the future needs of the business itself. You should identify the knowledge, skills, abilities, and the background and experience that are necessary to enable the person to perform successfully in the job. And you should also note merging business trends and considerations that will place new demands on the position. After you've done all this, you should draft a description of the job and a career-development plan for the would-be successor. You should then use what you've written down to screen potential family candidates for the senior position.

Besides appropriate training and background, you need to assess the candidate's ability to function well in critical managerial areas, such as strategic planning, decision making, problem solving, leadership, and interpersonal and organizational communication. One good technique for assessing the candidate's capabilities in these areas is to describe a few hypothetical situations and ask how the candidate would handle them.

If the business does not adhere to strict standards of merit in promotions, or if there is only one possible successor, you may not have a say in the selection. What if you don't believe that person is well qualified? As the mentor, you can—and should—take the issue up with the parent, again using the job description as an objective test.

More often than not, parents will, on some level, be aware of their children's shortcomings. But they may not know how to confront the problem. One solution you can suggest is to transfer responsibilities in any areas in which the successor is deficient to another employee. You can point out that this can be an opportunity for the business owner to elevate the status of relatives or key nonfamily managers who might be disappointed that they were not chosen as successor.

After the successor has been selected, there are a number of roles you should assume as the mentor. They include:

Career strategy advisor—providing general guidance and insight on the types of opportunities and experiences that the advisee should pursue.

Individual development counselor—charting a specific career development plan that the advisee should follow in his or her formal process of development.

Sponsor/mediator—making sure that the advisee gets the type of assignments essential for development.

Monitor—evaluating ongoing performance so that the advisee can make further progress.

Role model—furnishing an example that the advisee can learn from and emulate.

Organizational analyst—explaining the dynamics of the company and its "politics" to the advisee.

Liaison—introducing the advisee to key players inside and outside the company, including bankers, suppliers, and customers.

You should work out a plan with the business owner and his or her successor that sets benchmarks and intervals for reviewing progress. As long as your advisee is developing on schedule, you should gradually withdraw from the process.

A mentoring assignment well done pays off. Mentoring is an opportunity to shore up your relationship with both generations of ownership; if you do a good job, you can elevate your personal status and influence in the firm. And to the extent your mentoring ensures future growth and profitability of the family business, you maximize your own job security and any profit-based compensation you receive.

— Edwin T. Crego Jr.

Retiring

Install safeguards before you leave

Owners must protect their retirement income with legal guarantees, payout requirements, and financial restrictions on the next generation. These don't imply lack of trust; they constitute smart planning.

"T RUST IN GOD, but tie your camel first" is an old Sufi proverb that family business owners should heed when considering an ownership transfer. Even when giving the business to your children or selling it to them, you should exercise extreme care and negotiate safeguards that will protect you and your spouse from a disastrous loss of income. Your successors should understand that such precautions do not imply lack of trust or love but are necessary in case things go wrong after the transaction is completed—because they often do.

Most ownership transfer plans involve some form of deferred payout, which creates a risk that promised and expected funds may not be collected. Often the seller transfers stock in exchange for an interest-bearing installment note. Or he may be given a supplemental pension plan with payments to be funded by future earnings of the business. Whatever the terms of the transaction, the sellers take on some risk—and the business owner facing retirement wants security, not risk.

There are a number of security measures that sellers can insist on to legally ensure that the proceeds from a sale or income from a pension will not be interrupted. The hard call is: How far can you go to protect yourself without strangling the golden goose? If you put liens on all business assets to secure collateral, that may prevent the company from obtaining needed capital and defeat your purpose, which is to perpetuate the family business and secure your future income.

Of course, the owner can reduce or eliminate the risk of non-payment by pre-funding the transaction. He can begin setting corporate cash aside for himself well before the sale is to take place. Five-to-seven year lead times in succession can also help the owner assemble and groom the next generation of owner-managers.

One way to pre-fund the arrangement is through a supplemental pension plan used in conjunction with a grantor or "rabbi trust" (so named because the first IRS ruling on such trusts involved a retirement fund for a rabbi). Most family business owners, unfortunately, are not foresighted enough to set up such funds in advance. Or they find better things to do with income from the business that, at the time, seem to be wiser investments.

For business owners who do not want to place burdensome liens on the company but do want to protect their retirement income, there are some alternative ways in which they can secure their rights. These legal security devices are much the same as the ones used by any lender, which is, in effect, what the seller holding an installment note becomes.

1. Personal guarantees from the buyers. If the kids are not willing to put up their house or bank account or car as collateral, then they are not ready to be entrepreneurs. By insisting on such guarantees, the parent gives his successors a strong incentive to keep the business on course.

2. Compensation/bonus caps. The first two or three years will be the toughest for the new owners. If they expect to take the same income out of the company as the parents did, to equal the parents' life-style right away, they may not be able to make a go of it. To keep sufficient cash in the company and to be sure the new owners have a long-term view, the parents may want to have a provision in the sale contract requiring the new owners to maintain existing compensation levels for two or three years or to restrict bonuses and perks.

Of course, the level of compensation established for the new owners should be fair. It should cover the jobs that they had been doing before the sale and will continue to do afterward, plus an increment for any new responsibilities that they assume following the sale.

3. Restrictions on dividends during the deferred payout period. If the business is a C corporation, it's unlikely that it pays dividends. However, if it is an S corporation—

as many family companies are—stockholders often receive dividends to pay income taxes on the profits that are passed through to them. The sellers in this case may want a provision in the agreement that prevents larger dividend distributions until the new owners have finished paying for the business.

4. Measures to restrict the buyers from taking on new debt. In the event of a business default, some methods of deferring payment in a sale have a higher claim on the business's assets than others. It is therefore in the seller's interest to prevent the buyer from taking on debt that might subordinate what is owed on the installment note.

The holder of an installment note that is secured with collateral is typically in a more senior position to collect money owed than a general creditor (such as the participant in a supplemental pension plan). On the other hand, the company's bank may require the business to maintain a specific debt-equity ratio in order to avoid having the bank call inventory loans, working capital loans, or other borrowing. If the ownership transfer is structured as a long-term installment note, this additional debt may tip the debt-equity ratio unacceptably and result in a not-too-friendly visit from the banker.

In contrast, bankers view a supplemental pension plan as a junior obligation that is subordinated to their loans. In their debt-equity calculations, the pension plan is often considered to be "above-the-line equity" instead of long-term debt. So if the bank objects to a long-term installment note, the owner who wants to be sure the business remains viable may have no choice but to opt for the non-qualified pension plan, which offers less protection in a default because it is not secured by any collateral.

Even if the bank raises no objections, sellers will want to install other devices to protect what is owed on the note. In any default, the sellers usually occupy a second position after the company's regular lines of credit. They may therefore want to prevent the new owners from incurring further indebtedness that subordinates them to a third or fourth position on collateral. In the sale agreement, they will typically ask the new owners to pledge that existing lines of credit will not be expanded without their (the sellers') consent for as long as they remain creditors of the company.

If the seller still has personal guarantees on any corporate indebtedness, those guarantees should be removed before the sale or as part of the sale agreement. If for some reason they cannot be removed, the buyers should pro-

Reduce the risk of nonpayment by using the same security devices used by lenders.

vide indemnifications which assure the seller that they (the new owners) will cover any claims against him by a third party—even though such guarantees may be difficult to enforce once the business has changed hands.

One caveat: Don't expect a bank to automatically accept substitute guarantees from the new owners. It may take a banker several years, and many visits, before he develops the same confidence in the new owners that he had in the old.

5. Establish cash-flow coverage requirements for the deferred payout period. The sellers, of course, have a stake in seeing that cash flow in the business is adequate to pay off a note. The sale agreement should establish a mutually agreed upon coverage requirement. If cash flow falls below that, it would constitute a default by the buyers.

Usually, the sellers require the buyers to maintain the company's historical cash flow, which can be determined by the accountants. But there are a number of different ways of calculating cash flow. It is important to determine cash flow—earnings before depreciation and interest payments on mortgage and other borrowing, and taxes (EBDIT). The company should be obliged to maintain at least 1.0 times EBDIT coverage. For greater security, some banks and other lenders require 1.25 to 1.5 times EBDIT.

A seasonally low cash flow can accidentally trigger a default. The accountants can usually spot such trends in historical cash flow or they can sample cash flow in selected time periods. Then the sellers can have written into the sale agreement the criteria for judging when the business will be in default—for example, four or more quarters below the norm.

The cash-flow coverage requirements normally factor in the indebtedness to the sellers. The more that the new owners pay to sellers as tax-deductible expenses (in royalties, consulting fees, as income from a supplemental pension plan, or compensation for a non-compete clause) the better their company's cash flow picture and the easier it will be to meet the EBDIT requirement.

However, too many payouts of that sort can be a burden to the business. Keep in mind that the purpose is not to make the requirements so tough that the new owners will fail.

6. The holders of long-term notes should have the right to review the company's financials periodically. Set whatever period you like, but make sure the books will be accessible.

7. Put stock in escrow until the buyer pays off debts related to the buyout. This is fairly standard practice. Typically, the attorney for the seller or an escrow agent holds the stock until the debt is paid. If there is a business default, this presumably makes it easier for the seller to reclaim ownership of the business.

But this "stock pledge" does not prevent the buyers from dramatically changing the financial condition of the business. By the time the former owners take back the stock, it may be too late to save the company. Also, this security device is of no use when the former owners have gifted the stock to their successors and receive their income through a nonqualified retirement plan.

8. Get the new owners to sign a non-compete covenant. If the business doesn't succeed under the new owners, they should not have the option of being able to leave and set up shop elsewhere, taking advantage of the experience they have gained at the old owners' expense. This may seem to be a heartless provision for parents to insist on when they wish their children well. But it is not uncommon to see family vendettas in which offspring purposely set up competing firms to drive their parents or siblings out of business.

9. Require the new owners to carry life and disability insurance. If the new owners die suddenly or are disabled, the former owners may have to step back in. With the proceeds of insurance that has been collaterally assigned to them, the former owners can be assured of collecting any amounts due them. Insurance thus prevents one tragedy (the new owner's death) from becoming two (the former owners' loss of everything).

10. Prohibit the new owners from selling assets, making acquisitions, or getting into an entirely new line of business. The buyout agreement should keep the new owners focused on productively using the assets they have acquired and discourage them from spinning off assets for quick profit. The same goes for acquisitions and expansions.

Some owners approve of such risk-taking, at least within limits, and may not care to protect themselves against them in the agreement. However, the risk-averse owner will want to ensure that the new owners pay him off before embarking on any corporate expansion or acquisition program.

Although this list of security devices is not exhaustive, it underscores the importance to the sellers of getting up-front protection in the transaction. Some changes in the company's bylaws may also be required if the sellers are to retain a minority interest.

For example, the seller could amend the bylaws to include a "supermajority" provision that would require more than a simple majority for approval of changes in the direction of the business. If, for example, Dad retained 20 percent of the stock, such a provision could require a vote of at least 81 percent of all stockholders for major decisions. Such a provision could, in effect, give the minority holders a veto over a sale, merger, or recapitalization.

Another option is to have a "windfall provision" in the agreement, so that if the new owners sell the business within a few years for more than they paid for it, they would have to share the excess proceeds with the former owners.

If the seller feels the need for such guarantees, however, it may be that neither he nor the buyer is yet ready for the transaction. The process of negotiating these security devices often brings out hidden concerns of the people sitting on both sides. When an owner wants to perpetuate a family business, he has to cut some strings. There is a fine line between what is a fair and justifiable measure to protect the retirement income of the aging owner and his spouse and what is demanded because the owner is not really willing to let go.

— Mike Cohn

Resources

GENERAL

Mind Your Own Business and Keep It in the Family, by Marcy Syms. Mastermedia Ltd., New York, 1992.

Generation to Generation: Life Cycles of the Family Business, by Kelin E. Gersick, John A. Davis, Marion McCollum Hampton, and Ivan Lansberg. Harvard Business School Press, Boston, 1996.

Your Family Business: A Success Guide for Growth and Survival, by B. Benson, E.T. Crego, R.H. Drucker. Dow Jones-Irwin, Homewood, IL, 1990.

Keeping the Family Business Healthy: How to Plan for Continuing Growth, Profitability, and Family Leadership, by John Ward. Jossey-Bass, San Francisco, 1987.

Inside the Family Business: A Guide for the Family Business Owner and His Family, by Léon Danco. Cleveland Univ. Press, 1981.

The Family in Business, by Paul F. Rosenblatt, Leni de Mik, Roxanne Marie Anderson, Patrica A. Johnson. Jossey-Bass, San Francisco, 1985.

Family Business Sourcebook, by Craig Aronoff and John Ward eds. (collection of articles). Omnigraphics, Detroit, 1990.

LEADERSHIP

Born to Power: Heirs to America's Leading Businesses, by Jan Pottker. Barrons, 1992.

Smart Growth: Critical Choices for Business Continuity and Prosperity, by Ernesto Poza. Jossey-Bass, San Francisco, 1989.

Corporate Bloodlines: The Future of the Family Firm, by Barbara B. Buchholz and Margaret Crane. Carol Publishing Co., New York, 1989.

Global Perspectives on Family Business, by the Family Business Center. Loyola University Chicago, 1994.

BUSINESS AND FAMILY

Working With the Ones You Love: Conflict Resolution and Problem-Solving Strategies for a Successful Family Business, by Dennis T. Jaffe. Conari Press, Berkeley, CA.

Cultural Changes in Family Firms: Anticipating and Managing Business and Family Transitions, by W.G. Dyer Jr. Jossey-Bass, San Francisco, 1986.

How to Run a Family Business, by Michael Friedman and Scott Friedman. Betterway Books, Cincinnati, 1994.

How to Make the Transition from an Entrepreneurship to a Professionally Managed Firm, by Eric G. Flamholtz. Jossey-Bass, San Francisco, 1986.

How Entrepreneurial Couples Are Changing the Rules of Business and Marriage, by Sharon Nelton. Wiley, New York, 1986.

So That Your Values Live On: Ethical Wills and How to Prepare Them, by Jack Riemer and Nathaniel Stampfer eds. Jewish Lights Publishing, Woodstock, VT. *How to Compile and Publish Your Family Business History,* by Cindy Chapman. Oregon State University, Corvalis, 1993.

Keeping the Family Business Healthy, by John Ward (audiotape). Jossey-Bass, San Francisco, 1987.

Making Your Family Business Outlast You, by Craig Aronoff and John Ward (audiotape). Nation's Business, Washington, D.C.

ORGANIZATIONS:

American Arbitration Association, 140 West 51st St., New York, NY 10020-1203. Phone: 212-484-4000.

OPERATIONS

Up Against the Wal-Marts: How Your Business Can Prosper in the Shadow of the Retail Giants, by Don Taylor and Jeanne Smalling Archer. American Management Association, New York, 1994.

ORGANIZATIONS:

Society of Competitor Intelligence Professionals, 818 18th St. N.W., Suite 225, Washington, D.C. 20006. Phone: 202-223-5885.

continued on next page

Resources *continued*

ADVISORS AND CONSULTANTS

Creating Effective Boards for Private Enterprises, by John Ward. Jossey-Bass, San Francisco, 1991.

ORGANIZATIONS:

Attorneys for Family Held Enterprise, PO Box 188, Millersville, PA 17551. Phone: 717-871-9005.

SUCCESSION

Passing the Torch: Succession, Retirement, and Estate Planning in Family Owned Businesses, by Mike Cohn. McGraw-Hill, New York, 1992.

Beyond Survival, by Léon Danco. Cleveland University Press, 1982.

The Hero's Farewell: What Happens When CEOs Retire, by J. Sonnenfeld. Oxford U. Press, 1988.

Family Business Succession: The Final Test of Greatness, by Craig E. Aronoff and John L. Ward. Business Owner Resources, Marietta, GA.

Your Final Test for Success, by Mike Henning. Henning Family Business Center, Effingham, IL, 1992.

Preparing...Just in Case, by Patricia A. Frishkoff and Bonnie M. Brown. Oregon State University, Corvalis, 1992.

Preserving Family Wealth & Peace of Mind, by Loren Dunton and Kim Ciccarelli Banta. Probus Publishing, Chicago, 1994.

Transfering the Privately Held Business, by Irving L. Blackman. Blackman Kallick Bartelstein, Chicago.

Someday, All This Will Be Yours, by Connecticut Public Television and E. McKeon (videotape). Massachusetts Mutual Life Insurance Co., Springfield, MA, 1993.

INSTRUCTIVE FAMILY BUSINESS HISTORIES

Sam Walton: Made in America, My Story, by Sam Walton with John Huey. Doubleday, New York, 1992.

The Nordstrom Way: The Inside Story of America's #1 Customer Service Company, by Robert Spector and Patrick D. McCarthy. John Wiley & Sons, New York, 1995.

Crisis in Candyland: Melting the Shell of the Mars Family Empire, by Jan Pottker. National Press Books, Bethesda, MD, 1995.

Steinway & Sons, by Richard K. Lieberman. Yale University Press, New Haven, CT 1995.

The Crain Adventure: The Making and Building of a Family Publishing Company, by Robert Goldsborough. NTC Publishing, Lincolnwood, IL, 1992.

Father Son & Co.: My Life at IBM and Beyond, by Thomas J. Watson. Bantam Books, New York, 1990.

The Fords: An American Epic, by P. Collier and D. Horowitz. Summit Books, New York, 1987.

Marriott: The J. Willard Marriott Story, by Robert O'Brien. Deseret Book Co., Salt Lake City, UT, 1979.

Friends in High Places: The Bechtel Story, by Laton McCartney. Simon & Schuster, New York, 1992.

Riding the Runaway Horse: The Rise and Decline of Wang Laboratories, by Charles C. Kenney. Little Brown & Co., Boston, 1992.

Cargill: Trading the World's Grain, by Wayne G. Broehl Jr. University Press of New England, Hanover, NH, 1992.

Newhouse: All the Glitter, Power, and Glory of America's Richest Media Empire and the Secretive Man Behind It, by Thomas Maier. St. Martin's Press, New York, 1994.